A Student's Guide to CHINESE AMERICAN Genealogy

Oryx American Family Tree Series

A Student's Guide to CHINESE AMERICAN Genealogy

By Colleen She

Oryx Press
1996

Copyright 1996 by The Rosen Publishing Group, Inc.
Published in 1996 by The Oryx Press
4041 North Central at Indian School Road
Phoenix, Arizona 85012-3397

Printed and bound in the United States of America.

∞ The paper used in this publication meets the minimum
requirements of American National Standard for Information
Science—Permanence of Paper for Printed Library Materials,
ANSI Z39.48, 1984.

Library of Congress Cataloging-in-Publication Data
She, Colleen.
    A student's guide to Chinese American genealogy / by Colleen She.
      p. cm. — (Oryx American family tree series)
    Includes bibliographical references and index.
    ISBN 0-89774-980-4
    1. Chinese Americans—Genealogy—Handbooks, manuals, etc.
  2. Chinese Americans—Genealogy—Bibliography. 3. Chinese
Americans—History. I. Title. II. Series: Oryx American Family
Tree.
E184.C5S47   1996
929'.1'089951073—dc20   96-17158
                                                 CIP
                                                 AC

Contents

Chapter 7. Oral History, 130

Chapter 8. Your Final Result, 154

Glossary, 160

Index, 164

The Lee family of Washington, DC, kick off their 1947 family reunion with a traditional Dragon Dance. The Lees, whose Chinese American family members numbered more than 22,000, traced their genealogy back 2,500 years.

Chapter 1
Making History Come to Life

Exploring a genealogy can be an exciting and rewarding enterprise. During the process, you play the roles of detective and historian. Finding the names, birthdates, and places of residence of your ancestors is only one aspect of genealogy. In addition, you will have the opportunity to explore creative applications of your newly acquired knowledge. Reconstructing family history requires both analytical skill and intuition. Historical events rest in the realm of imagination: only the vestiges remain and it is up to you to synthesize available data.

This guide is designed to help you start to uncover not only your own ancestry, but also the past of Chinese Americans as a group. Genealogy is also an opportunity for self-discovery. A family history may become the start of something more ambitious, such as biography or historical fiction. Some of the most prolific Chinese American novelists, such as Maxine Hong Kingston and Amy Tan, have drawn much from their personal experiences as well as the experiences of other family members and ancestors. We are the result of generations upon generations of lives; each of our ancestors has become a small part of ourselves.

Creating a genealogy is difficult but rewarding work. There is little vitality in the process unless you apply your imagination to the raw data. Each chapter in this volume is designed to make genealogy come to life. Because many Chinese language sources are inaccessible to those who do not know the language, we will give you a sense of what can be available if you study the Chinese language or enlist the help of a Chinese-speaking relative. We will explore ways of creating a genealogy using your creativity. There are a number of avenues you can explore without consulting books.

The final product of genealogical research always has a particular scope, varying in the extent of horizontality or verticality. A horizontal genealogy does not go far back in time, whereas a vertical genealogy emphasizes chronological depth. A horizontal genealogy might detail the lives of a few selected ancestors. A vertical genealogy attempts to trace numerous generations, with less emphasis on particular people. Let's say you are interested in creating a vertical genealogy and in the process discover that there is an ancestor you wish to know about in greater depth. At this point, a change in your original plan may be necessary. You may, for instance, wish to transform a genealogy into a biography or a novel. Who knows what you might accomplish?

Remembering Your Origins

As a Chinese American, you may feel culturally American, but have you ever wondered what it might be like to transport yourself back in time? Perhaps your Chinese ancestors were farmers, or Confucian literati. Whoever your remote ancestors were, a part of them is in you.

Think of yourself as an archaeologist in search of a picture of the past. You find pieces here and there. One piece of information is like a potsherd (a broken piece of pottery). Like an archaeologist, you will probably find only part of the original artifact. Your information will be scattered about in different places. Some of it will fit together into a logical picture, but no matter what, there will always be missing information. It is important not to be discouraged by this.

Archaeologists reconstruct their artifacts based on available pieces. After they have a few major pieces, they infer the rest by extrapolating. You will need to do the same. Chinese culture has provided sizable material artifacts, especially written documents. Although not all of them can be examined in this book, ancient Chinese culture has left for us an array of paintings, scrolls, tombstones, and inscriptions—enough to occupy a scholar for life.

In 1946, Chinese American children salute the American flag before classes at the Commodore Stockton School in San Francisco's Chinatown.

As with written records, it could be argued that material objects do not speak for the average person. Such artifacts resulted from the patronage of wealthy members of society. This is true for many cultures. Yet, we rely heavily on these artifacts to understand the past. Although many people have not left written documents for us, your search for ancestors can still be a fascinating project as you examine material artifacts they created. In finding out about your past, you are creating your own web of significance. As you read written documents, be aware of the biases that might affect an author's observations.

Your genealogical adventure begins in the United States and goes back to China. The answers to the following questions will provide a historical context for your genealogy.

- Were my great-great-grandparents, great-grandparents, grandparents, or parents the first gen-

eration to immigrate to the United States?
* Where in China did my ancestors come from?
* When did my ancestors come to the United States?

Learning the Chinese Language

Your exploration of your family history will no doubt lead you to resources in the Chinese language. You may already speak Chinese at home, with your parents or grandparents. This skill will serve you well as you begin your research. Elderly relatives, for example, may be more comfortable speaking in Chinese when you interview them. The more comfortable an interviewee is, the more likely he or she is to open up and share important details of his or her life.

Knowledge of written Chinese is an even greater asset to the Chinese American genealogist. You will not only be able to read and understand records in Chinese, but you will also be able to write and request records from Chinese sources.

If you do not speak Chinese, don't despair, particularly if your goal is to trace your family's history in the United States. You will probably be able to do most of this research in English through American records. However, if you wish to do research in China, you may want to think about learning the language of your ancestors. You may be able to enlist the help of a Chinese-speaking parent or other relative, but if you want to do your research more independently—or just want to pick up a new language—consult some of the books on Chinese language listed in the **Resources** of this chapter. The Chinese language is one of the world's oldest and most beautiful. It has influenced the writing systems and vocabularies of the Japanese, Korean, and Vietnamese languages. Unfortunately, it is also complex and quite difficult to learn. But the rewards will be tremendous. For one thing, more people in the world today speak Chinese than any other language, so your efforts will not be wasted. Although the majority of Chinese people (Han) use the official dialect (Mandarin), regional dialects are preferred by various minority groups. However, they share the same set of standard written characters. Therefore, genealogical materials from all

Historically, only noble families could afford to trace their genealogies. This undated photo depicts a Chinese noble family on the steps of their home.

over China will be accessible to you if you can read standard characters.

The Chinese language is currently taught in more than 100 American universities and colleges, and Chinese book collections can be found in twice as many public and academic libraries, especially in states with large Chinese communities such as New York, California, Texas, Massachusetts, Florida, Michigan, Illinois, and Hawaii. Interest in the Chinese language has been constantly increasing during the last three decades. Thus, while in 1960 only 18,000 American university and college students registered to learn Chinese, in 1970 the number increased to 62,000, in 1980 it jumped to 114,000, and in 1990 it reached 195,000.

The Problem with Written Sources

Inscriptions, autobiographies, official histories, and any other written sources that are available today may not represent the voices and lives of all Chinese. For this reason, written sources should be approached with caution. In the past, most Chinese were farmers. They led lives that were important, though they rarely left written records about themselves. Written information was generally compiled by government officials. These official records give us only a glimpse into the world of the common people. Officials recorded events such as trials or local riots, often portraying the masses as rabble rousers. By the same token, Chinese officials praised people who embraced official state values. Because they were compiled by government officials, English-language documents relating to Chinese immigration also reflect an official bias.

As you proceed with your research, you will grow more skilled at approaching documents with a healthy degree of skepticism and awareness of their possible biases. You will be able to practice being a researcher, writer, and interviewer.

Resources

STARTING YOUR EXPLORATION

Bandon, Alexandria. *Chinese Americans.* **New York: Crestwood House, 1994.**

Emigration from China to the United States is chronicled, with information on how American Chinatowns developed. Also discusses current Chinese immigration.

Brownstone, David. *The Chinese-American Heritage.* **New York: Facts on File, 1988.**

The author focuses on the brutal discrimination faced by early Chinese immigrants who worked in American mines and ports. He demonstrates how this discrimination drove Chinese immigrants into restaurants, laundries, and domestic work.

Busuttil, Joelle. *Behind the Wall of China.* **Ossining, NY: Young Discovery Library, 1993.**

The geography, history, and daily life of China are described in this book.

Carpenter, Frances. *Tales of a Chinese Grandmother.* **Rutland, VT: C. E. Tuttle Co., 1973.**

An elderly Chinese grandmother shares traditional folklore with her grandchildren.

Cotterell, Arthur. *Ancient China.* **New York: Knopf, 1994.**

Learn more about the land of your ancestors from photographs of artifacts left behind by citizens of the world's oldest empire.

Daley, William. *The Chinese Americans.* **New York: Chelsea House, 1995.**

> An illustrated overview of the history and culture of Chinese Americans.

Filstrup, Chris. *China, from Emperors to Communes.* **Minneapolis: Dillon Press, 1983.**

> An overview of Chinese history, including art, traditions, and social life, plus a chapter on Chinese Americans.

Fong-Torres, Ben. *The Rice Room: From Number Two Son to Rock 'n' Roll—Growing Up Chinese-American.* **New York: Hyperion, 1994.**

> A prominent entertainment journalist recounts how, as a youth, he grappled with feelings of alienation from his parents and his Chinese heritage.

Hong, Maria, ed. *Growing Up Asian American.* **New York: William Morrow, 1993.**

> This anthology is a collection of thirty-three beautifully written stories and essays by Asian Americans who reflect on what it means to be Asian American.

Hoobler, Dorothy, and Hoobler, Thomas. *The Chinese American Family Album.* **New York: Oxford University Press, 1994.**

> The struggles and successes of Chinese immigrants in the United States are illustrated through oral histories, letters, diaries, and literary excerpts.

Kim, Hyung-Chan, ed. *Dictionary of Asian American History.* **Westport, CT: Greenwood Press, 1986.**

> An accessible reference guide to people, places, and events in the history of Asian Americans.

Kingston, Maxine Hong. *The Woman Warrior.* **New York: Knopf, 1976.**

A candid memoir of Kingston's childhood. She recounts her struggles to reconcile the "ghosts" of her Chinese heritage with her American upbringing.

Krull, Kathleen. *City Within a City: How Kids Live in New York's Chinatown*. New York: Lodestar Books, 1994.

Sze Ki Chau and Chau Liu, two recent arrivals to New York City's Chinatown, try to find a balance between Chinese tradition and life in a bustling American city.

Lee, Kathleen. *Tracing Our Chinese Roots*. Sante Fe: John Muir Publications, 1994.

Lee explores Chinese immigration to the United States and the traditions Chinese immigrants brought with them in fields such as art, cooking, medicine, and martial arts.

McCunn, Ruthanne Lum. *Chinese Proverbs*. San Francisco: Chronicle Books, 1991.

You may have heard your grandparents or other elderly relatives quoting Chinese sayings and wondered what they meant. This book explains the meanings of many popular Chinese sayings.

Morey, Janet Nomura, and Dunn, Wendy. *Famous Asian Americans*. New York: Dutton/Cobblehill, 1992.

A collective biography of fourteen prominent Asian Americans, including Chinese American tennis star Michael Chang and television journalist Connie Chung.

Morton, W. Scott. *China: Its History and Culture*. New York: Lippincott & Crowell, 1980.

Good introduction to China and its people from ancient times to the present day, accompanied by numerous photographs.

Ross, Frank, Jr. *Oracle Bones, Stars, and Wheelbarrows: Ancient Chinese Science and Technology*. Boston: Houghton Mifflin, 1982.

The ancient Chinese made amazing advances in the fields of astronomy, medicine, science, and engineering. Read about their incredible accomplishments.

Takaki, Ronald. *Ethnic Islands: The Emergence of Urban Chinese America.* **New York: Chelsea House, 1994.**

Photographs and illustrations accompany this text, which focuses on the development of Chinatowns and the contributions of Chinese Americans to American urban communities.

———. *Journey to Gold Mountain: The Chinese in Nineteenth-Century America.* **New York: Chelsea House, 1995.**

In this illustrated, easy-to-read volume, Takaki, an ethnic studies scholar, examines the harsh lives of Chinese immigrants who flocked to the United States in search of gold and riches.

Teague, Ken. *Growing Up in Ancient China.* **Mahwah, NJ: Troll Associates, 1994.**

What were your ancestors' lives like centuries ago? Teague examines schools, festivals, cities, the countryside, and other aspects of life to provide a glimpse of China in ancient times.

Wu, Dana Ying-Hui, and Tung, Jeffrey Dao-Sheng. *The Chinese-American Experience.* **Brookfield, CT: Millbrook Press, 1993.**

Chapters on Chinese American history and culture are supplemented with sidebars of primary source material, such as speeches, diaries, letters, songs, and poems.

Yu, Lin. *Cooking the Chinese Way.* **Minneapolis: Lerner, 1982.**

Learn how to prepare traditional Chinese foods with this colorfully illustrated cookbook.

ENCYCLOPEDIAS

"The Chinese" by H. M. Lai in *Harvard Encyclopedia of American Ethnic Groups*. Cambridge, MA: Harvard University Press, 1980.

Extensive presentation on China with map and bibliography.

"Chinese Americans" by L. Ling-chi Wang in *Gale Encyclopedia of Multicultural America* (vol. 1). Detroit: Gale Research, 1995.

Brief presentation of land of origin, Chinese history, and causes of immigration.

LEARNING THE CHINESE LANGUAGE

An, Jiang. *Chinese Word Book*. Honolulu: Bess Press, 1990.

More than 200 words are explained and illustrated. Both traditional and simplified characters are provided.

Aria, Barbara. *The Spirit of the Chinese Character*. San Francisco: Chronicle Books, 1992.

Chinese characters are ideograms—symbols that represent a thing or idea. This book introduces you to forty characters.

Chen, Janey. *A Practical English-Chinese Pronouncing Dictionary*. Rutland, VT: C. E. Tuttle Co., 1992.

It is virtually guaranteed that you will come across Chinese words in the course of your genealogical research. More than 15,000 words and their definitions and pronunciations are provided here.

De Mente, Boye Lafeyette. *Chinese in Plain English*. Lincolnwood, IL: Passport Books, 1995.

Romanized Chinese helps readers understand words used frequently in daily Chinese conversation.

Goldstein, Peggy. *Long Is a Dragon: Chinese Writing for Children.* **San Francisco: Chronicle Books, 1991.**

Learn how to write seventy-five Chinese characters by following detailed examples, and read about the history of the Chinese written language.

Scurfield, Elizabeth. *Chinese.* **Lincolnwood, IL: NTC Publishing Group, 1992.**

Pronunciation guides, cultural notes, grammar summaries, vocabulary charts, and other aids introduce the novice to this ancient and beautiful language.

FICTION

Chin, Frank. *Donald Duk: A Novel.* **Minneapolis: Coffee House Press, 1991.**

On the eve of the Chinese New Year in San Francisco's Chinatown, twelve-year-old Donald Duk attempts to deal with his comical name and his feelings for his cultural heritage. This fictional account depicts the challenges encountered by Chinese Americans as they try to assimilate in American society.

Gish, Jen. *Typical American.* **New York: Plume, 1991.**

Lai Fu comes to the United States to study to be an engineer. But soon he becomes Ralph Chang, and is joined by his sister Theresa. Together they forge new lives and experience their own version of the American dream.

Hagedorn, Jessica, ed. *Charlie Chan Is Dead: An Anthology of Contemporary Asian American Fiction.* **New York: Penguin, 1993.**

Diana Chang, Amy Tan, and Jeffrey Paul Chan are among the many Chinese American writers featured in this anthology. They explore contemporary themes and issues of identity.

Tan, Amy. *The Joy Luck Club.* **New York: Putnam, 1989.**

Stories about Chinese American mothers and daughters underscore the tension between first- and second-generation women. The mothers want their daughters to remain Chinese, yet they also want them to be successful; the thoroughly American daughters realize that they cannot ignore their Chinese heritage. This book was made into a movie; look for it on video.

Ward, Arthur Sarsfield. *Tales of Chinatown.* **Freeport, NY: Books for Libraries Press, 1971.**

This is a collection of fictional short stories: "The Daughter of Huang Chow," "Kerry's Kid," "The Pigtail of Hi Wing Ho," "The House of Golden Joss," "The Man with the Shaven Skull," "The White Hat," "The Dance of the Veils," "The Hand of the Mandarin Quong," "The Key of the Temple of Heaven."

Yep, Laurence. *The Lost Garden.* **Englewood Cliffs, NJ: J. Messner, 1991.**

Yep, a Chinese American who grew up in San Francisco's Chinatown, sold his first story for a penny a word when he was eighteen. His identity as Chinese American is an essential part of his writing. This book, a memoir, is a celebration of his family and his ethnic heritage.

———. *The Star Fisher.* **New York: Puffin Books, 1991.**

Yep tells the story of fifteen-year-old Joan Lee and her family, who move from Ohio to West Virginia in the 1920s.

———. *Thief of Hearts.* **New York: Harper Collins Publishers, 1995.**

This is a fictional account about a Chinese American. When the protagonist, Stacy, is paired with a Chinese girl at school who is accused of theft, she must come to terms with her own Chinese and American heritage.

Chapter 2
Being Chinese American

Chinese Americans, who number over 1,700,000, including Taiwanese, according to the 1990 U.S. Census, and more than 2,200,000 by unofficial estimation, constitute the largest and oldest Asian American group in the United States. They are settled mostly in the states of California, New York, Hawaii, Massachusetts, and Illinois and established well-known Chinatowns in the cities of San Francisco, Los Angeles, New York City, Honolulu, Boston, Chicago, and Seattle. However, Chinese Americans can be found in other states too. According to the latest census data, there is no state without some Chinese American presence. The 1990 U.S. Census also shows that more than 1,200,000 Chinese Americans have declared Chinese as their mother tongue, which represents about two-thirds of the total recorded Chinese American population and is a much higher percentage than other ethnic groups.

Chinese Americans have established hundreds of social, cultural, benevolent, political, artistic, athletic, and other organizations, associations and clubs, and have published numerous newspapers, journals, and books in Chinese, Chinese and English, or English. Although Taoism and Buddhism are the major traditional religions of China, a sizable percentage of Chinese Americans belong to Christian churches (Protestant and Catholic). Chinese cuisine is well known and appreciated outside of the Chinese American community. Equally popular are Chinese songs and dances, especially during the Chinese New Year celebrations.

An Overview of Chinese American History

The Chinese presence in America can be traced back to the

sixteenth through eighteenth centuries, but immigration officials recorded the first Chinese immigrants only during the 1820s.

The first period of mass immigration (1840s–1882) started with the arrival of several thousand Chinese peasants from southern China (the provinces of Guangdong and Fujian) who, like many other immigrants from various parts of the world, were attracted to the United States by the Gold Rush in California. They were followed by tens of thousands of immigrants who came as contract laborers to the American West, working in mines, in the construction of railroads, building irrigation systems, fishing and agriculture, and industry. Chinese immigrant women were employed in sweatshops in the textile industry. By 1880, the Chinese immigrant population reached 105,465 persons.

The second important period in Chinese American history (1882–1965) was a sad one. When the cheap labor provided by Chinese immigrants was no longer needed, and strong anti-Chinese sentiments were nurtured by labor forces who saw in the Chinese immigrants strong competitors, the U.S. Congress enacted harsh anti-Chinese immigration laws (for example, the Scott Act in 1888, the Geary Act in 1892, and the Deficiency Act in 1902) denying not only the entry of new immigrants, but also naturalization and civil rights even to those Chinese who already were established in the United States. The anti-Chinese laws were accompanied by brutal anti-Chinese riots in 1871 and 1885 in which dozens of Chinese workers were killed.

Small quotas of Chinese immigrants were permitted during the 1940s and 1950s. These immigrants were usually either war brides of American servicemen or refugees from Communist China.

During this period, the Chinese population in America decreased from 105,465 recorded in 1880 to 77,504 in 1940.

The negative effects of the past were reversed by the

Immigration and Naturalization Act of 1965. Basic rights were restored to Chinese Americans, including the right to family reunification with relatives from abroad. In the following three decades, hundreds of thousands of Chinese immigrants were admitted to the United States. They came from Communist China, Taiwan, Hong Kong, and war-torn Indochina (during the 1970s), and included several thousand intellectuals, scientists, engineers, and clerical and skilled workers, as well as other categories eager to find economic opportunities and a better future for their children. At the end of the 1970s, the Chinese American population consisted of almost 400,000 people.

Chinese Americans are active participants in all aspects of American life today. Thirty-three percent are involved in professional and technical activities, over 15 percent work as managers and administrators, about 15 percent as sales and clerical workers, 7 percent as forepeople and craftspeople, and the rest as small business owners, service workers, farmers, farmworkers, and a broad variety of other jobs.

Many young Chinese Americans are remarkable achievers in American high schools, colleges, and universities, and become professionals in the fields of medicine, science and technology, arts, teaching, writing, and many other areas.

Reasons for Emigration from China

Widespread hunger and poverty, political instability, and a resentment of foreign influence were among the reasons many Chinese people immigrated to the United States.

Leadership in China in the late nineteenth and early twentieth centuries was characterized by an increasing decentralization of governmental power. The population was increasing rapidly, and the amount of available productive land was inadequate to feed the population. The government, unable to cope with the population explosion and food shortage, came to be viewed as weak by the Chinese people. The government's stance was further weakened by the growing interference of European countries in China's affairs. The defeat of China in several wars against the West

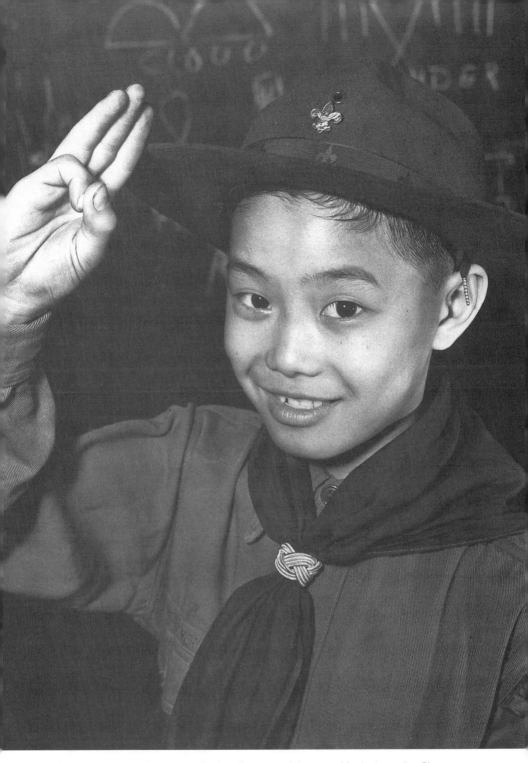

Chinese Americans became involved in all aspects of American life. In 1942, this Chinese American boy was a member of Boy Scout Troop 150.

resulted in China's forced agreement to extraterritoriality—a condition requiring China to concede certain areas to foreign economic and political control. For example, in Shanghai, the French government controlled the city's court system and police force. Foreign laws applied to Chinese people within these territories, but foreigners in the same areas were not subject to punishment if they broke Chinese laws.

In response to the increasingly weak central government, military strongmen set up their own regimes in China's provinces. Military fortifications were built in the countryside. This time in Chinese history is known as the Warlord Period.

Southern China was most directly affected by Western influence. Europeans and Americans were eager to purchase silks, jewels, porcelain, and tea from the Chinese. However, there was little that the Chinese wanted to buy from Westerners. In the early 1800s, seeking to tip the trade balance more in their favor, the British began to smuggle opium into China in defiance of Chinese law. The Opium War of 1839–1842 was a result of the conflict between China and Great Britain over the opium trade. China lost the war, and the southern province of Guangdong was impoverished and destabilized as a result.

Some Chinese turned against their own people as coordinators of the "coolie" trade business. Coolie was the term used to refer to Chinese peasants who worked as indentured servants in Southeast Asia, Peru, Cuba, Hawaii, and other areas. The term was also applied to laborer immigrants in the continental United States. The origin of the word *coolie* is uncertain. It may come from two Chinese characters, *ku* and *li*, which mean "bitter" and "labor" respectively. Another theory is that it is an anglicized version of the Hindi word *quli*, which is thought to be related to a word meaning "wage laborer." The coolie trade was also known as the "credit-ticket" system. Labor brokers, often Chinese themselves, lured young Chinese men with promises of the wealth that awaited them outside of China. Kidnapping was sometimes used when promises failed to entice potential emigrants. The coolie trade mainly occurred between the fifteenth and nineteenth centuries. A strong Western presence in Canton, the capital of Guangdong province, and the predominance of the coolie trade there might explain why the majority of the first wave of emigrants from China were Cantonese. Peasants were also prompted to emigrate from the southern Chinese provinces of Guangdong and Fujian because of population pressures, ethnic warfare, the concentration of land in the hands of the upper classes, and other factors that made their lives miserable.

Early Chinese Immigrants

The first large wave of Chinese immigration to the United States took place during the mid-nineteenth century. Between 1850 and 1890, more than 100,000 Chinese immigrants arrived in the United States, many of them attracted by the Gold Rush in California.

The development of the mining and railroad industries in the western states gave rise to a demand for cheap labor. Chinese men came to the United States for economic betterment, leaving their families behind. Many intended to stay in the United States only temporarily, hoping to return to China after having amassed a fortune.

Chinese men were recruited by the thousands as laborers for American railroad companies. Even though technically they weren't indentured servants, these laborers were also called coolies. Mining, lumber, sugar, and railroad companies were the main hirers of coolie labor in the Americas. Chinese men would leave their families behind to take on years of contracted work, often to find themselves laboring in inhuman conditions similar to those endured by African American slaves. In fact, it was the waning of the slave trade that made Chinese contract workers so appealing to American and British companies. Coolies "ate bitterness" in an alien country far from their families and the tightly knit communities of their homeland.

The saying "You don't stand a Chinaman's chance" originates from the fact that coolies were used to perform the dangerous task of laying dynamite to clear the way for

Chinese Americans played a pivotal role in the building of the transcontinental railroad. The above engraving depicts Chinese workers laboring in California's Sierra Nevada mountain range.

railroads. Even though more than 12,000 Chinese workers helped to build the western portion of the Central Pacific Railroad—the first transcontinental railroad in the United States—no Chinese workers were listed as present when the gold and silver spikes were driven in Promontory, Utah, in 1869 to mark the railroad's completion. Chinese unskilled laborers were largely responsible for the building of the western half of the transcontinental railroad in the 1860s and 1870s. Once that project was completed, the Chinese workers who remained and those who hoped to come to the United States were unwelcome. Companies were discouraged from bringing over any more contracted workers: to do so was considered aiding and abetting unskilled immigrants who would take jobs away from American workers.

If you have not been able to determine which of your ancestors first set foot in the United States by asking living relatives, you should point your compass westward to California. This is where most early Chinese immigrants settled. Statistics compiled during the census of 1870 reveal that of the 63,199 Chinese in the United States, 49,227 of them lived in California. By comparison, there were only 748 Chinese in New York, the second largest Chinatown during this period. The discovery of gold in California in 1848 precipitated a large wave of Chinese immigration. Several thousand Chinese men mined the California goldfields; others made their way to gold strikes in Nevada, Colorado, British Columbia, and other western regions.

When mining was no longer a promising endeavor, Chinese immigrants pursued other livelihoods, such as agriculture; shoe, cigar, and textile manufacturing; the fishing industry; coal and copper mining; and service industries. Chinese immigrants also became restaurant, tailor shop, and laundry owners in small mining towns across the American frontier. These three occupations were known as the "Three Knives" by the Chinese, a reference to the misery associated with the work.

Although a vast majority of Chinese Americans still live in

California, a substantial number also live in Hawaii. In 1789, the first Chinese came to Hawaii in the employ of a British captain on his way from China to British Columbia. In Hawaii, a vast resource of sandalwood was discovered, and a growing number of Chinese became involved in shipping the valuable wood back to Mainland China.

Hawaii's real draw for the Chinese was the sugar trade. The southeastern Chinese province of Guangdong, from which many Chinese Americans can trace their roots, was China's major sugar-producing area. In 1852, 195 contracted laborers were shipped from Fujian province (just north of Guangdong) to Hawaii to work in sugar mills. The need for Chinese laborers was caused by a decrease in Hawaii's indigenous population resulting from exposure to European diseases and poor working conditions. Sugar production continued to grow throughout the nineteenth century. Between 1852 and 1900, 50,000 Chinese immigrants came to Hawaii.

Hakka, or Kejia, immigrants, who spoke the Hakka dialect, were among the Chinese immigrants who settled in Hawaii during the 1850s and were involved in sugar cultivation and production. The Hakka had settled in Guangdong during the thirteenth century.

The draw to the continental United States was even stronger (remember that Hawaii did not become a state until 1959). In 1852 alone, 20,000 Chinese landed in San Francisco. The initial influx dropped to between 2,000 and 9,000 per year over the next decade. Hawaiian Chinese are not as homogeneous as those who immigrated to the continental United States.

Mandarin has been the "official" language of China since the imperial era. Today it is spoken by 70 percent of the population of China. One out of six Chinese in China calls Mandarin his or her mother tongue. It is native to northern China, especially in and around the city of Peking.

Cantonese is spoken by about 64 million people, making it the third largest language in China (after Mandarin and English). Named after the city of Canton, it is used mostly in the Guangdong and Kwangsi provinces in southeastern China, as well as in Hong Kong. Because the majority of Chinese émigrés to the United States came from southeast China, there are many Cantonese speakers among Chinese Americans.

If you are Hawaiian Chinese, keep in mind that although civil records began in Hawaii in 1853, they were quite sporadic until 1896, when such things as birth, marriage, and death certificates fell to the custody of the U.S. Department of Education.

First Communities

The first Chinese communities grew in northern California, primarily in San Francisco and Oakland. Although "Chinatowns" existed in many major metropolises, they were never as visible as those in San Francisco and New York. The first Chinese settlers in northern California retained a strong tradition of clan and kinship ties, common in southern China. They often settled in areas where they had clan or family connections. Particular surnames predominated in each of the Chinatowns across the United States. Chinese immigrants organized themselves into *huiguan*, or district associations, according to their region of origin. In San Francisco, several *huiguan* formed the Chinese Six Companies, an organization designed to provide mutual aid and protection to Chinese Americans.

During the first half of the twentieth century, young Chinese Americans began to leave urban Chinatowns for other city neighborhoods or suburban areas. For example, the Sunset District in San Francisco is an example of an area that became home to many Chinese Americans who left the older Chinatown district. As the population of urban Chinatowns grew older, the young men who remained there had to seek their brides elsewhere. These changes in the settlement patterns of Chinese Americans accelerated after World War II.

The Board of Chairmen of the Chinese Six Companies conferred in 1946, in what was believed to be the first photo ever taken of the group. The organization provided assistance to Chinese immigrants and Chinese Americans, worked to resolve conflicts between tongs (Chinese fraternal organizations), and represented members when they encountered difficulties with local and national authorities.

Tongs and Tong Wars

In the 1850s, recent Chinese immigrants to California organized various kinds of community groups. One such group was the *huiguan*, which was made up of immigrants who came from a common area in China. The *huiguan* were active in civic affairs, writing letters to state and local governments to address discriminatory policies, and representing power and discipline in San Francisco's Chinatown. The *huiguan* often came into conflict with another kind of Chinese organization, the tong.

The word tong means meeting hall, but in America it came to stand for fraternal organizations that fought to protect Chinese immigrants from discrimination on the job and in the streets. Continuing a tradition in China, tongs operated in secret, and had a more mob-like approach than the *huiguan*. Membership in a tong was determined less by district of origin or kinship than by the ability to pass secret initiation rites. The most famous tong was Zhigongtang (Chee Kung Tong), which was a direct outgrowth of a secret society that operated in China.

Tongs in America were especially popular among the lower classes. Educated merchants were more likely to join the *huiguan*. Working-class Chinese Americans had a rough life, and the power in numbers provided by tong membership made these groups appealing. Having been ostracized by their American host communities, tongs took their power wherever they could. They became organizers of illegal businesses such as gambling, drug dealing, and prostitution. Soon, certain tongs started up rivalries among each other, fighting for turf much like today's urban gangs. Violent street rumbles were fought, called "tong wars" by the American popular press and literature. Although these "wars" were greatly sensationalized in the public mind, long feuds led to a feeling of danger both to communities at large and within Chinese neighborhoods.

It should be noted that, throughout the years of tong power, tongs in Hawaii remained peaceful defenders of anti-Chinese injustice. On the North American continent, tong violence raged especially rampant during the 1910s and 1920s. A temporary truce was declared among North American tongs in 1925. In 1933, the U.S. government arrested and deported many remaining tong members.

Tongs are still active in many Chinese American communities. Today, they no longer operate in secret or act as underground mobs. Instead, they devote their efforts and funds to helping the members of their neighborhoods, and to extending a welcome to newcomers from China.

Official Discrimination

Chinese immigrants have always faced a number of challenges in the United States. Cultural barriers inhibited immediate assimilation into the mainstream American community. For years, they also faced government-sanctioned discrimination. There were laws, for example, preventing Chinese from marrying Caucasian Americans, and a person who was 50 percent Chinese was considered to be Chinese by the U.S. government. During the late nineteenth and early twentieth centuries, acts were passed in Congress that forbade Chinese to immigrate to the United States. Many Americans believed that the Chinese were flooding the job market and causing unemployment to rise.

The fear that Chinese immigrants were stealing American jobs brought about a state of near-panic. Chinese workers' non-Western clothing and hairstyles caused Americans to see them as evil and mysterious.

One of the earliest businesses in which Chinese immigrants thrived was laundering. They succeeded in this useful trade everywhere they went, from San Francisco to Brooklyn. Americans resentful of their successes spread gossip about their hard-working Chinese neighbors. Wild accusations reached such a fervor in several parts of the country that riots and arson were directed against Chinese residents.

In one of the most horrifying incidents of anti-Chinese hate crime during this period, sixty-two Chinese miners were murdered near Snake River, Idaho, in 1875 by whites dressed as Native Americans. Even local governments tried to stop the economic success of Chinese Americans by the passage of anti-Chinese laws. For example, in 1870, San Francisco levied a tax against laundries. The proprietor of a laundry was taxed $2 per delivery horse. Any launderer who used no horses would be taxed $15. This law seems to make no sense until one realizes that Chinese laundries used no horses. Ultimately, practically every one of the laws was declared unconstitutional when challenged.

A business often associated with Chinese Americans is the operation of laundries. Gin Shee Quong, the mother of four children, operated a laundry in the 1930s in Ashland, Ohio.

Chinese Women Immigrants

Chinese women immigrated in much smaller numbers than Chinese men in the second half of the nineteenth century. This was due to several factors.

Traditional Chinese culture encouraged women to stay at home, marry, and have children. Women were expected to marry men from the same or neighboring village. It was not generally acceptable for a woman to work outside the home, much less leave that home for another country.

The practice of foot-binding is an example of a way in which traditional Chinese culture kept women close to their families. Women were physically unable to be on their feet for very long because their feet were bound tightly to make them small and pointed. An unnaturally tiny foot was considered very beautiful. The practice of foot binding was also an indication of social standing. Families who needed their daughters to work the fields could not afford to bind their daughters' feet. Thus, bound feet were a sign of being from a wealthy family. Unfortunately, this practice kept women in constant pain and restricted their mobility.

Money was also a factor in keeping Chinese women at home. The fare to the United States was expensive, and few families could afford to send more than one family member.

Most male Chinese immigrants left their wives and daughters behind in China. They expected the separation to be temporary. Many waited to leave until their wives were pregnant, and hoped to father more children on future visits home. This practice was encouraged by the sons' parents, who wanted to ensure that the money their sons earned came back to China to support their extended families.

A few women did buck tradition and leave China for the United States—sometimes with their husbands, sometimes alone. Life for these new immigrants was often extremely difficult. They were isolated in Chinese American communities with few other women. It was hard for them to learn English, and their lives consisted of backbreaking work in Chinese-owned businesses. Thousands of Chinese women also worked in sweatshops in the garment industry in American cities. Many women fortunate enough to join their husbands soon found themselves virtual prisoners of tong wars. One of the tongs' favorite strategies was abducting their rivals' wives. In some areas it was unsafe for women ever to leave the house; many of these women saw other females only once a year, at the Chinese New Year celebration.

Poor Chinese girls were sometimes sold into prostitution. Sadly, these girls made up the large majority of the first Chinese women immigrants to the United States. This brought all Chinese women under suspicion of being prostitutes. In 1875, the U.S. government acted on these suspicions and passed federal laws in 1875 to bar most Chinese women from entering the United States. Later laws continued to restrict the entrance of Chinese women. In fact, in 1890, after fifteen years of the exclusion of Chinese women, the ratio of Chinese men to women in the United States was only 27:1. Consequently, the number of Chinese American children was very low even though Chinese immigration had been going on for fifty years.

Restrictions on the immigration of Chinese women kept the Chinese immigrant community from mirroring the development of European immigrant communities in the United States. In those communities, men had also tended to immigrate first and then sent for their wives and children. However, in the case of the Chinese immigrants, women were forbidden to enter the United States at exactly the time that male immigrants had established themselves and would have been preparing to send for their wives and children. Chinese exclusion laws stifled the natural development of the Chinese American community. Male Chinese immigrants with families back in China often had to endure separation from their families if they hoped to remain in the United States. Men who had been bachelors when they immigrated were often unable to find suitable brides in the United States and could not form families.

Chinese Exclusion Laws

In 1875, the Page Law was passed by the federal government. This law forbade the entrance of Chinese contract laborers, felons, and women imported for the purpose of prostitution. As it turns out, this law had almost no effect on the number of men who entered the United States. Women, on the other hand, were stringently barred from entry. In 1876–1882, Chinese men entering the country numbered about 100,000. During that same period, only 1,500 women were granted entry.

The U.S. government, reacting to popular opinion, worked to keep unskilled Chinese laborers out. In 1880–1881 a treaty was signed with China that allowed the United States the right to "regulate, limit, or suspend" the immigration of laborers from China. The terms of the treaty were slated to take effect in 1882, with the passing of the Chinese Exclusion Act. In China, there was great resentment about the treaty. Determined to circumvent it, 50,000 Chinese managed to slide in under the wire in 1881–1882. Only 219 of these were women.

Under the Chinese Exclusion Act, Chinese merchants, tourists, teachers, and students were allowed to enter the United States. Likewise, the wives of merchants and the educated were sometimes allowed in, while Chinese wives of American citizens were not. The Exclusion Act decreased but did not stop Chinese immigration. In the 1870s the Chinese influx had reached an all-time high of over 120,000, nearly twice the number in the previous decade. That number decreased to 60,000 in the 1880s.

Seeing that the 1882 act had not curtailed the influx of uneducated men, the U.S. government passed the Scott Act in 1888. This law made it impossible for a Chinese laborer who left the United States ever to return. The law discouraged Chinese immigrant men from visiting or fetching their wives who remained in China, unable to emigrate. The result was that thousands of families were separated, some never to be reunited. In 1924, the Immigration Act denied entry to practically all Asians.

Twentieth-Century Immigration

From a genealogical standpoint, one of the most fascinating moments of Chinese American history occured in 1906. There was a huge earthquake and fire in San Francisco during that year. Among the enormous damage was the loss of many thousands of immigration and naturalization records. Here was an opportunity for Chinese Americans to buck the system. Thousands of Chinese people forged certificates stating that they had been born in the United States. This made them legal citizens. These people then went to China, gathered up three or four younger men or boys, and returned to the United States, signing a statement that these were their "sons." Any child of an American citizen is by law also a citizen. The youngsters who were brought to the United States via this method were referred to as "paper sons." It took a while for customs officials to catch on to this scheme. Within a few years, however, entrance requirements became stricter than ever, particularly at Angel Island, a port of entry in San Francisco Bay. Ten percent of the Chinese who made the journey—including many with a legitimate right to enter—were turned away from Angel Island because the immigration officials had become so suspicious.

In 1943, the U.S. Congress repealed all Chinese exclusion laws. Chinese were granted the right of naturalization and a small immigrant quota (105 per year). The reason for these changes was World War II. Americans realized that the Chinese and Japanese peoples were not identical. Sadly, the government turned against the Japanese living in the United States. The Chinese became trusted friends. To galvanize this image, approximately 20,000 Chinese men and women served in the U.S. army in World War II, and many others worked at highly skilled jobs such as engineering and designing. Resident Chinese were allowed to become U.S. citizens. After World War II ended, several thousand Chinese women were admitted to the country as war brides of U.S. servicemen. The Chinese American population in the United States contributed significantly to the war effort, helping to change public opinion.

China went through turmoil during the first half of the twentieth century, when civil war erupted between the Nationalists, led by Chiang Kai-shek, and the Communists, led by Mao Zedong. During the 1940s, the Communists fought the Nationalists for political control of China. In 1949, the Nationalists fled to the island of Taiwan and set up a regime in Taipei. Just after the defeat, the Nationalists believed that they would be able to take back their homeland. This did not happen. Both the government of the People's Republic of China (PRC) and the government of the Republic of China in Taiwan (ROC) still claim to be the sole legitimate government of the Chinese.

The People's Republic of China formed political relations

The U.S. Refugee Act of 1953 resulted in an influx of immigrants seeking to escape Communist China. Many of these refugees were professionals and intellectuals who contributed their knowledge and skills to American science, education, and industry. Above, Wan Ju Pan Chan, widow of a Chinese college professor, arrives in New York with her son and three adopted boys.

with the Soviet Union, but contact with the United States was condemned. Immigration to the United States was closed off to the majority of Chinese.

When the Communists took power in 1949, about 5,000 highly educated Chinese in the United States sought asylum. Asylum was granted partly as a show of disapproval of the new Communist regime. It was also a feather in America's cap to be the country of choice for China's educated elite. From 1953 through 1967, various refugee acts were passed by the United States to help Chinese people escape communism. The most important came in 1965, when the Immigration Act itself was changed to eliminate national origin as a basis for determining entry. During that period some 23,000 educated Chinese sought political asylum in the United States. They were allowed to stay, but only under the watchful eye of the Federal Bureau of Investigation. The nation was gripped with a terror of Communist infiltration.

The first premier of Communist China, Mao Zedong, was determined to have a classless society. In the years before 1966 he set up a campaign to rid China of its long traditions of literacy, thought, and art. This campaign was called the Cultural Revolution. First, Mao closed schools, and urged young Chinese to join the Red Army's youth organizations instead of continuing with a traditional education. Soon teachers were being persecuted, along with doctors, artists, and others with specialized skills who might be considered elites. Cities underwent violent purges of their intelligensia.

Mao later expressed regret that the revolution had been so violent and excessive. Nevertheless, his ideology had taken hold of many official minds. Even after Mao left office in 1969, a group called the Gang of Four continued censorship and cultural purging until its members were imprisoned near the end of 1976.

During this period, many educated Chinese fled for their lives to the United States. The huge influx of educated, highly skilled Chinese workers is often referred to as a "brain drain," indicating that China's loss of its intellectual and artistic population was a boon to the United States. During

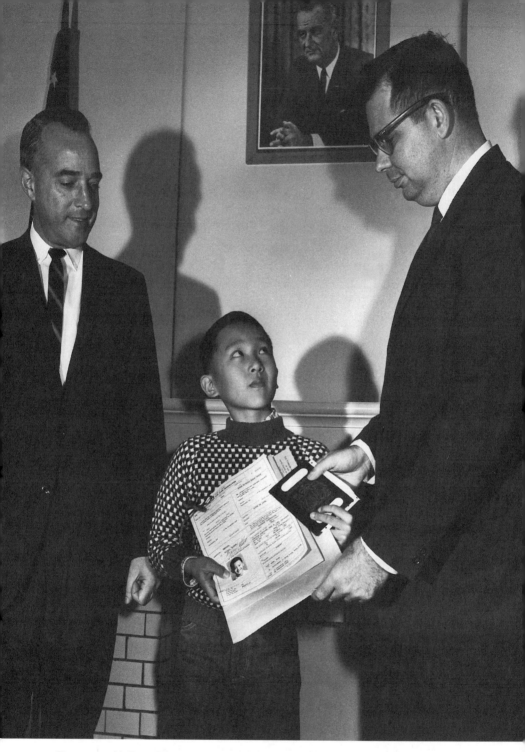

Eleven-year-old Gene Wong was the first recipient of a U.S. visa in Taiwan when U.S. immigration policies changed in favor of Asian immigration in 1965. Since the act was passed, more than 5 million Asian immigrants have entered the United States.

the early years of the Cultural Revolution, some 23,000 well-educated middle-class Chinese entered the United States as political refugees. Immigration Acts in 1976 and 1977 reduced the number of Chinese professionals allowed in. In this legislation, certain professions (such as health care) were removed from the list of fields in need of practitioners. Entrance exam requirements, both in the profession and in English, became more stringent. In addition, American employers had to be able to prove that they had made an effort to hire someone in the United States.

Because Canton was under British rule, immigration continued throughout the twentieth century. Chinese who had established themselves in the United States led the effort to bring in their relatives. The Chinese who had fled to Taiwan were also able to immigrate. Until U.S. President Richard Nixon revived diplomatic relations with Mainland China during the 1970s, Taiwan was effectively considered "China." Cultural exchange between the United States and Taiwan took the form of such things as student exchange programs.

Chinese living in Taiwan often came to the United States to seek educational advancement. During the 1950s, many Chinese immigrants acquired advanced degrees in science and engineering. After receiving degrees in highly technical fields, they were unwilling to return to Asia, for there were fewer career opportunities there to match their skills, and the standard of living was significantly lower than in the United States. They also cited fear of a Communist takeover of Taiwan. They stayed and found work in the United States, often becoming prosperous citizens.

Since 1965, Chinese entrance to the United States has been steadily increasing. President Jimmy Carter officially recognized the People's Republic of China in 1979. Diplomatic ties were established with PRC and broken with ROC (Taiwan). PRC became a member of the United Nations Security Council.

After the United States reestablished diplomatic ties with Mainland China, student exchange programs were set up.

Many recent immigrants from Mainland China have been students. Taiwan continues to send students to the United States in pursuit of higher education. The end of British authority in Hong Kong in 1997 has resulted in a flood of immigration to both Canada and the United States by those wishing to avoid life under a Communist government.

Successful Chinese Americans

Chinese Americans have distinguished themselves since their first years in the United States. The first person of Asian ancestry to win a state office in the mainland United States was Wing F. Ong. Ong came from China in 1918 at the age of fourteen. Before being elected to the Arizona House of Representatives in 1943, he worked as a houseboy for the governor of Arizona and owned and operated a grocery store.

Chinese Americans are esteemed scholars, scientists, and professionals, stars of stage and screen, and winning athletes. Just a few of the many Chinese Americans who have achieved distinction in their fields are tennis star Michael Chang; figure skater Tiffany Chin; actors Bruce Lee, Brandon Lee, Ming Na Wen, Russell Wong, Jackie Chan, and B. D. Wong; directors John Woo and Ang Lee; cellist Yo-Yo Ma; television journalist Connie Chung; authors Amy Tan, Maxine Hong Kingston, and Gus Lee; architect I. M. Pei; and diplomat Wellington Koo.

The Fight Against Discrimination

Unfortunately, the 1875 Snake River incident was not the last case of discrimination and violence against Chinese Americans. In the 1880s, violence against Chinese workers became more organized. In 1885, Chinese coal miners in Wyoming Territory were driven from their homes, beaten, and shot at when they declined to join white workers in a strike. That same year, more than 600 Chinese residents of Tacoma, Washington, were forcibly removed from the town and deposited at a nearby railroad station on a stormy night. A string of other violent incidents occurred throughout the

Pacific Northwest and California in the 1880s. Violence against Chinese immigrants had its origins in racism and American workers' fear of competition for jobs. It is not a coincidence that violence against Chinese workers has been particularly acute during periods of economic depression in the United States.

In employment, education, housing, and other areas of their lives, Chinese Americans had to fight for their rights. Discrimination was never accepted by Chinese immigrant communities—they fought for justice. For example, in June 1867, Chinese workers stopped work on the transcontinental railroad in protest of the fact that Chinese workers, who worked tediously long days and were beaten by their over-seers for lapses, did not receive meals or lodging with their wages, while European American workers received board in addition to wages. The Chinese workers were forced to end their strike when the railroad company stopped bringing them food. Chinese immigrant workers in a San Francisco garment factory went on strike in 1875, as did workers on a Hawaii plantation in 1891.

In addition to strikes, legal action was also a method of redress used by Chinese immigrants. Hundreds filed suit in American courts, mostly in response to immigration exclu-sion laws. Chinese immigrants also used the courts to fight for their right to U.S. citizenship and for the right to main-tain their livelihoods. Laundries, especially in San Francisco, faced especially difficult challenges in the 1870s and 1880s. Ordinances passed by the city government attempted to restrict the number of laundries and their ability to conduct business. In New York, Chinese laundry owners struggled against governmental discrimination as well as the power of Chinatown institutions such as the Chinese Consolidated Benevolent Association. This struggle led to the formation of the Chinese Hand Laundry Alliance in the early 1930s to protect the rights of laundry owners.

The harsh treatment of Chinese workers in the United States, the exclusion of new Chinese immigrants, and the abusive attitude of immigration officials toward visiting

Chinese (who should not have been affected by the exclusion laws) prompted a boycott of American goods in China in 1905. The boycott was ended after the Chinese government stepped in, but did succeed in gaining recognition for the Chinese plight and fostering political solidarity among Chinese immigrants in the United States.

In the 1980s, the economic rise of Japan and an influx of Southeast Asian refugees were among the factors that contributed to increased violence against Asian Americans. One of the most horrific cases of anti-Asian violence was the 1982 murder of Vincent Chin in Detroit. Chin, a twenty-seven-year-old draftsman who was engaged to be married, was at a nightclub with some friends. Two white men, Ronald Ebens and his stepson, Michael Nitz, picked a fight with the group in the club. All of them were kicked out of the club when a fistfight broke out. Ebens and Nitz retrieved a baseball bat from the trunk of their car and began to chase Chin and his friends. They caught up with Chin in front of a McDonald's restaurant and beat him brutally with the bat. He died four days later. It is suspected that the killers' motivation might have been that they mistook Chin as Japanese and blamed the Japanese for the problems in the American automobile industry, in which Nitz and Ebens worked.

The light sentences received by Chin's murderers outraged the Asian American community. They and non-Asian citizens mobilized to impose harsher sentences. While they were successful in having the case retried, Nitz and Ebens were eventually acquitted. Unfortunately, six years later the opportunity arose for the lessons learned in the Vincent Chin case to be applied. In 1989, twenty-four-year-old Chinese American Jim Loo was murdered in Raleigh, North Carolina, by two brothers who thought he was Vietnamese. A Jim Loo American Justice Coalition was immediately organized. Although one of the brothers received a light sentence and was paroled in only six weeks, the other brother was sentenced to thirty-seven years in prison. The Coalition announced that justice had been achieved.

The Chin and Loo cases point to the fact that Chinese Americans still face racial barriers and must fight for justice and equality. They also point to the incredible resiliency, determination, and commitment to justice that characterize the Chinese American community. In a touching example, Vincent Chin's mother, Lily Chin, overcame her limited knowledge of English to speak out publicly about the unjust way in which her son's murder was handled by the courts.

Ethnic Diversity

Just as Chinese American identity has many definitions, so too does Chinese identity. As you trace your roots back to the land of your ancestors, you will uncover a whole new world. Some of it may be familiar to you because of your Chinese heritage. Some of it may be very foreign to you.

Chinese people are about as diverse as Europeans. The Chinese mainland comprises thousands of communities with distinctive local cultures. Although the Chinese people share a common dialect (Mandarin), regional dialects were, until recently, the preferred medium of communication. Fortunately, all Chinese dialects share the same set of standard written characters. This means that genealogical materials from all over China can be universally understood by those literate in Chinese.

Most Chinese people belong to the Han ethnic group. A significant number of others who were lumped into one "Chinese" category by United States immigration officials may in fact have been members of various minorities. Perhaps you are descended from a so-called "minority" group. Beneath the all-encompassing term "Chinese" lies a world rich in diversity.

In modern-day China, people of the Han ethnicity make up about 94 percent of the population. The other 6 percent is a mix of more than fifty ethnic groups. The lifestyles of these peoples vary widely. Some, in fact, are indistinguishable from the Han or from each other except by language. The largest non-Han groups are the Zhuang, Manchu, and Hui. The nearly 16 million Zhuang occupy an area of

When researching your family history, keep in mind that your family may belong to one of China's many minority peoples who were simply categorized as "Chinese" by immigration officials. The Hakka are one of China's numerous minorities. This 1962 photo shows a Hakka farmer wearing the large ruffled hat characteristic of these residents of southern China.

southern China. The Manchu and Hui peoples, numbering nearly 10 million each, have long lived in the central and eastern portions of Mainland China. The Zhuang, Manchu, and Hui probably contributed the most non-Han Chinese immigrants to the United States. The Hakka people were also represented among Chinese immigrants, especially in Hawaii.

On the northeastern lobe of the mainland live the Uighur and their neighbors, the Kazakh. The Uighur practice agriculture, while the Kazakh are nomadic sheepherders.

National Minorities (non-Han) of China

Achang	Jing	Pumi
Bai	Jingpo	Quiang
Be'ang	Jino	Salar
Blang	Kazakh	She
Bonan	Kirgiz	Shui
Bouyei	Lahu	Tajik
Dai	Lhoba	Tatar
Dong	Li	Tibetan
Dongxiang	Lisu	Tu
Drung	Manchu	Tujia
Duar	Maonan	Uighur
Ewenki	Miao	Uzbek
Gaoshan	Moinba	Va
Gelo	Mongol	Xibe
Hakka	Mulam	Yao
Hani	Naxi	Yi
Hezhen	Nu	Yugur
Hui	Oroqen	Zhuang

(Source: 1991 *Cambridge Encyclopedia of China*)

Although their lifestyles are very different, the two peoples are closely connected in language and in their practice of Islam. Condensed into an area just north of the Zhuang's region, the Miao and Yao speak languages from an entirely different family. They are distinguished by living on steep hills, where they cultivate rice. Every few decades they wear out the land in the region and shift their entire villages.

The Mongols, spread across north central China, are linguistically related to the Uighur but practice Buddhism rather than Islam. This religion was brought from Tibet and adopted by the Mongols. The Dai people of the southwest, on the other hand, show influences from Thailand in their dress and the way they build their houses.

Chinese minority groups possess as rich a genealogical history as the Han Chinese. Many of China's emperors were not Han Chinese or were of mixed ancestry. These emperors were assimilated into Han Chinese culture. All official court documents were written in Chinese, and the emperors themselves spoke Mandarin fluently.

Resources

CHINA AND CHINESE HISTORY

Abel, Clarke. *1780–1826: Narrative of a Journey in the Interior of China.* **New York: Arno Press, 1971.**

This is a reprint of the 1818 edition of a travel diary. If you do not read Chinese, a good way to learn about ancient China directly is to read diaries of Westerners who traveled there. Many Western missionaries and journalists traveled to China during the nineteenth century.

Appel, Benjamin. *Why the Chinese Are the Way They Are.* **Boston: Little, Brown, 1973.**

Presents a history of dynastic China and the nineteenth-century invasions that weakened her and led to internal strife. Also discusses the rise of the Chinese Communists and the social and political life of China today.

Arlington, Lewis Charles. *Through the Dragon's Eyes.* **London: Constable & Co. Ltd., 1931.**

Arlington tells about his fifty years of experiences as a foreigner in the Chinese government service. Arlington was in China during an extremely turbulent time. The monarchy was effectively dismantled, and there was a great deal of talk among Chinese government officials as to what kind of new government needed to be established.

Beresford, Charles William De la Poer. *The Break-Up of China.* **New York: Harper, 1900.**

This book gives an account of China's commerce, currency, waterways, armies, railways, and politics at the turn of the century. You may stop to wonder how your ancestors were faring at this time if they were still in China.

Bonavia, David. *The Chinese.* **London: Penguin, 1980.**

Bonavia, a foreign correspondent, explores the contradictions and complexities of Chinese history, culture, politics, and society. Includes chapters on Chinese medicine, writers in China, and Chinese emigration.

Broomhall, Marshall. *The Chinese Empire: A General and Missionary Survey.* **London: Morgan & Scott, 1907.**

Much firsthand historical information about China was gathered by Western missionaries. Some of your ancestors may have been converted to Christianity by missionaries. If this is the case, you might be able to find their names through old church records. In the mid-twentieth century, the Communists forced all Western missions to return to their home countries. If missionary records survive today, they are probably kept in the country where the mission originated.

Buck, Pearl S. *China As I See It.* **New York: John Day Co., 1970.**

Pearl Buck has written a number of classic novels about China, including *The Good Earth.* Here she offers her own perspective on China.

Chiang Kai-shek, President and Generalissimo of the Republic of China: As Seen through the Eyes of Foreign Friends and Journalists. **Taipei: China Publishing Co., 1968.**

This is a compilation of addresses and lectures of General Chiang Kai-shek, who led a group of Nationalist Chinese to Taiwan when the Communist Party prevailed in China in 1949. You can learn from your parents whether your family stayed in Mainland China or went to Taiwan.

Terrill, Ross. *China in Our Time: The Epic Saga of the People's Republic from Communist Victory to*

Tiananmen Square and Beyond. **New York: Simon and Schuster, 1992.**

An examination of China's people, politics, problems, and successes during the last four decades.

FILMS AND VIDEOS ABOUT CHINA

China Commune. **Westinghouse Broadcasting, 1974.**

A look at life in the Kwang Li People's Commune in China. Provides a glimpse of the Communist system in action.

China Diary, **1989. Directed by Jin-hua Yang.**

A documentary that explores some of the recent changes since China opened its doors to the West. The filmmaker, a young Chinese woman raised during the Cultural Revolution, returned to China after a five-year absence.

China, Land of My Father. **New Day Films, 1980.**

A first-generation Chinese American, journalist Felicia Lowe, searches for the roots of her father's family in China. The film's climax is a touching family reunion with aunts, uncles, cousins, and a grandmother.

The Chinese Way of Life. **Aims Media, 1986.**

This video focuses on the rapid changes taking place in China, especially in rural areas.

Cities in China Series: Beijing. **University of California at Berkeley, 1980.**

Get a taste of the flavors of China's lively capital; its architecture, shopping centers, Tiananmen Square, a model school, and other interesting facets.

Cities in China Series: Suzhou. **University of California at Berkeley, 1980.**

Images from a Yangtze delta city, considered by some to be the center of Chinese culture.

Cities in China Series: Xian. **University of California at Berkeley, 1980.**

A history of the ancient imperial city of Xian on the Wei River, including the famous tomb of Xian's first emperor, buried with 6,000 terra cotta warriors, a Buddhist temple, and other architectural treasures.

Eat Drink Man Woman, **1994. Directed by Ang Lee.**

A widower who works as a chef does his best to raise his three daughters in this Taiwan-set film. A story of food, fatherhood, and family. For mature audiences.

Empire of the Sun, **1987. Directed by Steven Spielberg.**

A British boy in Shanghai is separated from his parents when Japan invades China at the beginning of World War II. Based on the autobiography by J. G. Ballard.

First Moon: Celebration of Chinese New Year. **New Day Films, 1987.**

This documentary depicts an exuberant fifteen-day Chinese New Year festival in a village 400 miles southwest of Beijing, featuring parades, costumes, dances, and ancestral worship.

The Good Earth, **1937. Directed by Sidney Franklin.**

A Chinese farming couple's lives are ruined by greed in the film version of Pearl Buck's classic novel.

The Great Wall, **1986. Directed by Peter Wang.**

A Chinese American family travels to China to trace their roots. The film documents their sense of culture shock. (In Mandarin Chinese.)

Growing Up in China. **Pictura Films, 1974.**

A film about education in China, showing children working, dancing, and singing.

Keep Fit, Study Well, Work Hard. **Churchill Productions, 1973.**

Accompany the filmmakers on a visit to a Chinese school, observing the system of discipline and group activities in which the children participate.

The Last Emperor, 1987. **Directed by Bernardo Bertolucci.**

This film is inspired by the true story of Pu Yi, the last emperor of China, who was crowned at age three. He was deposed during the Communist Revolution. Scenes in the movie were filmed in the Forbidden City. The film won nine Academy Awards, including best picture. For mature audiences.

Made in China. **Filmmakers Library, 1985.**

The filmmaker Lisa Hsia reflects on her Chinese heritage while living with relatives in China. Through animation, home movies, and live action footage, she chronicles her search for identity.

Raise the Red Lantern, 1991. **Directed by Zhang Yimou.**

A young educated woman is forced to become the fourth wife of a rich old man. The film portrays the workings of the mansion where the four wives live. The young wife falls in love with her husband's nephew, who has been enslaved by his uncle to work in his dye factory. The film is a feast for the eyes, with the rich colors of the dyes and artful views of the mansion's architecture. For mature audiences.

Small Happiness: Women of a Chinese Village. **New Day Films, 1984.**

Women from a village discuss love and marriage, childbearing, family relationships, and work.

CHINESE AMERICANS AND CHINATOWNS

Bales, Carol Ann. *Chinatown Sunday: The Story of Lilliann Der*. Chicago: Reilly & Lee Books, 1973.

A ten-year-old Chinese American girl describes her family and their life in a Chicago suburb. There are many well-known Chinatowns along both coasts of the United States. This book stands out from most in that it tells of the Chinese American experience in the American Midwest.

Brott, C. W. *Moon Lee One: Life in Old Chinatown, Weaverville, California*. San Diego: Great Basin Foundation, 1982.

Chinese have settled all over California. Many moved outside the cities into small agricultural communities. University research libraries in California often contain specialized studies on specific geographical regions where Chinese have settled.

Carter, Frances. *Exploring Honolulu's Chinatown*. Honolulu, HI: Bess Press, 1988.

For genealogical research, you should familiarize yourself with the geographical details of your ancestors' Chinatown. This is a guide to Honolulu's Chinatown. If you cannot visit it, you can at least get an idea of what it is like today.

Chan, Sucheng. *Asian Americans: An Interpretive History*. Boston: Twayne Publishers, 1991.

A comprehensive study of the Asian American experience. Chan examines the history of Chinese American settlement, discrimination faced by Chinese Americans, and the unique experiences of second-, third-, and fourth-generation Chinese Americans.

Chen, Hsiang-Shui. *Chinatown No More: Taiwan Immigrants in Contemporary New York*. Ithaca, NY: Cornell University Press, 1992.

Recent waves of Chinese immigration have been from both the Chinese Mainland and Taiwan. Immigrants from Taiwan today often come to the United States having already established themselves economically. They do not live in congested urban areas, but choose instead a life in the comforts of suburbia.

Chen, Julia I. Hsuan. *The Chinese Community in New York: A Study in Their Cultural Adjustment, 1920–1940.* **San Francisco: R and E Research Associates, 1974.**

New York City's Chinatown was the second-largest, trailing behind San Francisco. Chinese in New York not only settled in Manhattan, but populated areas such as Queens. New York's unique geographical layout created pockets of ethnicity where Chinese immigrants formed cohesive communities. Chen presents her findings on these communities.

Chew, Ron, ed. *Reflections of Seattle's Chinese Americans: The First 100 Years.* **Seattle: University of Washington Press, 1994.**

A history of Chinese Americans in the state of Washington, with information on immigration, settlement, and contributions of Chinese Americans.

Chin-shan ko chi/Songs of Gold Mountain: Cantonese Rhymes from San Francisco Chinatown. **Berkeley: University of California Press, 1987.**

Most of the first Chinese immigrants to the United States were from Canton. They formed a strong community in San Francisco. Much of the culture was centered around the mining industry. The immigrants called San Francisco Chin-shan, or Gold Mountain. Immigrant cultures tend to rally around song for social support and acceptance. This volume contains 220 of the folk songs from *Songs of Gold Mountain (Chin-shan ko chi)*, published in 1911 and 1915.

Chinatown, DC: A Photographic Journal. **Washington, DC: Asian American Arts and Media, Inc., 1991.**

Your relatives may have established themselves in this medium-sized immigrant community.

Chinatown Teen Post. Los Angeles, CA: Chinatown Teen Post, 1978.

First-generation Chinese American immigrants have a voice all their own. This is a collection of writings by the youth of Chinatown. It is an example of a Chinese American youth newspaper.

Fong, Timothy P. _The First Suburban Chinatown: The Remaking of Monterey Park, California_. Philadelphia: Temple University Press, 1994.

Chinese Americans of southern California have formed a tightly knit community in Monterey Park, a suburb of Los Angeles. These days, much of it serves a low-income Chinese community.

Fong-Torres, Shirley. _San Francisco Chinatown: A Walking Tour_. San Francisco: China Books and Periodicals, 1991.

A walking tour of the most famous American Chinatown, along with information on social life and customs.

Genthe, Arnold. _Genthe's Photographs of San Francisco's Old Chinatown_. New York: Dover Publications, 1984.

This book features photos of nineteenth-century landmarks in San Francisco's Chinatown, some of which are still standing today.

Kiang, Ying Cheng. _Chicago's Chinatown_. Lincoln, IL: Institute of China Studies, 1992.

An examination of the Chinese in Chicago.

Kim, Hying-chan. _Asian American Studies: An Annotated Bibliography and Research Guide_. Westport, CT: Greenwood Press, 1986.

This bibliography will lead you to sources that can answer your specific questions about Chinese Americans. You might just browse through the bibliography to see if there are topics that strike you as interesting or pertinent to your family.

Knox, Jessie Juliet. *Little Almond Blossoms: A Book of Chinese Stories for Children.* **Boston: Little, Brown, 1907.**

Like Western culture, Chinese have fairy tales and parables to teach young children lessons in morality. This collection includes photographs of Chinese children in California.

Krull, Kathleen. *City Within a City: How Kids Live in New York's Chinatown.* **New York: Lodestar Book, 1994.**

Although New York is often thought of as a cosmopolitan city, ethnic segregation and provincial attitudes have often kept one group isolated from another. Chinatown is a world of its own.

Kwong, Peter. *Chinatown, New York: Labor and Politics.* **New York: Monthly Review Press, 1979.**

Many Chinese Americans worked hard in blue-collar jobs. This book discusses Chinese American participation in trade unions.

Lai, Chen-Yan David. *Chinatowns: Towns Within Cities in Canada.* **Vancouver: University of British Columbia Press, 1988.**

Descriptions and illustrations of Chinese communities in Canadian cities, such as Toronto.

Law, Ruth. *Dim Sum: Fast and Festive Chinese Cooking.* **Chicago: Contemporary Books, 1980.**

Recipes for special occasions, notes on Chinese kitchen equipment, and methods of preparation.

McCunn, Ruthanne Lum. *Chinese American Portraits: Personal Histories, 1828–1988.* **San Francisco: Chronicle Books, 1988.**

The Chinese immigrant and Chinese American experiences are told through oral history.

Museum of Chinese in the Americas
70 Mulberry Street
New York, NY 10013

Chinese immigrants have a long history not only in the United States, but also in Mexico, Canada, and Central and South America. This museum—formerly the Chinatown History Museum—has expanded to become a repository of information on Chinese around the world. Exhibit items include two pairs of shoes—one pair, four inches long, covered a Chinese mail order bride's bound feet; the other pair, eight inches long, covered her freed American toes.

Reit, Seymour. *Rice Cakes and Paper Dragons.* **New York: Dodd, Mead, 1973.**

Text and photographs introduce a girl of New York's Chinatown, her family, and their celebration of Chinese New Year.

Salter, Christopher L. *San Francisco's Chinatown: How Chinese a Town?* **San Francisco: R & E Research Associates, 1978.**

A study of the architecture in San Francisco's Chinatown. Many Chinatowns have undergone urban renewal. For more information about Chinatowns from the architectural and urban renewal perspective, call the Chinatown Resource Center at 415-984-1454.

Sheu, Chuen-Jim. *Delinquency and Identity: Juvenile Delinquency in an American Chinatown.* **New York: Harrow and Heston, 1986.**

Many people stereotype Chinese American youths as outstanding students. Unfortunately, Chinese American urban youths have not always been able to escape the plight of other urban youths across the United States.

Sung, Betty Lee. *The Adjustment Experience of Chinese Immigrant Children in New York City*. Staten Island, NY: Center for Migration Studies, 1987.

A focus on Chinese American children and the process of cultural assimilation.

Takaki, Ronald. *Strangers from a Different Shore: A History of Asian Americans*. Boston: Little, Brown, 1989.

Takaki, a noted scholar, examines the history of Chinese and other Asian immigrant groups and the challenges they faced.

Thompson, Richard H. *Toronto's Chinatown: The Changing Social Organization of an Ethnic Community*. New York: AMS Press, 1989.

Chinatowns in Canada have sprung up recently in anticipation of Hong Kong's return to Mainland China in 1996. Immigration to the United States and Canada has become a trend among educated people, who are considered economic immigrants.

Tung, W. L. *The Chinese in America, 1820–1973: A Chronology and Fact Book*. Dobbs Ferry, NY: Oceana Publications, 1974.

Covers major themes in immigration, settlement, and contributions to the United States. Appended with relevant documents.

Warner, Joie. *A Taste of Chinatown: America's Native Chinese Cuisine*. New York: Crown Publishers, 1991.

Chinese food prepared in American restaurants has taken on its own unique features. This book provides examples of typical Chinese dishes and explains how they are prepared in Chinatowns.

Waters, Kate. *Lion Dancer: Ernie Wan's Chinese New Year*. New York: Scholastic Inc., 1990.

Describes six-year-old Ernie Wong's preparations, at home and in school, for the Chinese New Year celebrations and his first public performance of the lion dance.

Wong, Bernard. *Patronage, Brokerage, Entrepreneurship, and the Chinese Community of New York*. New York: AMS Press, 1988.

Many business practices have been brought by Chinese immigrants to the United States. Chinese who first immigrate set up businesses with other Chinese because of similar cultural expectations and business practices.

Wong, Ho Leun. *An American Chinatown*, edited by the Great Basin Foundation. San Diego: The Great Basin Foundation, 1987.

The so-called Inland Empire of southern California has never been considered a region heavily populated by Chinese. As this volume demonstrates, however, Chinese Americans have left their traces even in Riverside, California.

Yee, Paul. *Tales from the Gold Mountain: Stories of the Chinese in the New World*. New York: Macmillan, 1989.

A collection of stories about Chinese immigrants overcoming prejudice and adversity.

Yu, Connie Young. *Chinatown, San Jose, USA*. San Jose, CA: San Jose Historical Museum Association, 1991.

The Silicon Valley in California has attracted many Chinese immigrants. San Jose has become a hub for educated Chinese in technical fields.

Yung, Joy. *Chinese Women of America: A Pictorial History.* **Seattle, WA: University of Washington Press/ Cultural Foundation of San Francisco, 1986.**

Pictures and text tell the story of Chinese women immigrants to the United States.

FAMOUS CHINESE AMERICANS

Buck, Ray. *Tiffany Chin: A Dream on Ice.* **Chicago: Children's Press, 1986.**

Chin, a Chinese American figure skater, competed in the 1984 Winter Olympics. Read about her life and her dream of winning a gold medal.

Dell, Pamela. *I. M. Pei: Designer of Dreams.* **Boston: Houghton Mifflin, 1993.**

The architect I. M. Pei is known for his use of glass and concrete in his designs. This book covers his family background, education, and career.

———. *Michael Chang: Tennis Champion.* **Chicago: Children's Press, 1992.**

Chang was the youngest man ever to win the French Open tennis tournament.

Fox, Mary Virginia. *Bette Bao Lord: Novelist and Chinese Voice for Change.* **Chicago: Children's Press, 1993.**

Fox describes Lord's love of her homeland and her attempt to bridge the Chinese and American cultures.

Gan, Geraldine. *Lives of Notable Asian Americans: Arts, Entertainment, and Sports.* **New York: Chelsea House, 1995.**

Read about a few of the many areas in which Asian Americans have distinguished themselves.

Malone, Mary. *Connie Chung: Broadcast Journalist.* **Hillside, NJ: Enslow Publishers, 1992.**

Chung is a pioneer in network television news, having achieved success in a field where minorities and women have faced many barriers. This book describes her family's emigration from China and her accomplished career.

Say, Allen. *El Chino.* **Boston: Houghton Mifflin, 1990.**

This book is a biography of Bill Wong, a Chinese American who became a winning bullfighter in Spain.

FILMS AND VIDEOS ABOUT CHINESE AMERICANS

Chan Is Missing, **1982. Directed by Wayne Wang.**

This detective story is set in New York City's Chinatown.

Chinese Roots, **1994. Directed by Donald Young.**

A group of Chinese American young adults decide to research their family histories. They use the National Archives and census and immigration records to find out about their families' lives in the United States. Then they embark on a trip to China to visit their ancestral villages. In the course of their research, they come to understand and appreciate the experiences of their parents and grandparents.

Dim Sum: A Little Bit of Heart, **1984. Directed by Wayne Wang.**

A tale of Chinese Americans in San Francisco, focusing on the relationship between a mother and daughter.

The Dragon Wore Tennis Shoes. **Diane Li Productions, 1975.**

Children and adults dress in elaborate costumes to participate in the Chinese New Year parade in San Francisco's Chinatown.

Freckled Rice. **National Asian American Telecommunications Association, 1985.**

The story of a boy in Boston's Chinatown, starring J. P. Wing and Douglas Lee.

The Golden Mountain on Mott Street. **Carousel, 1968.**

A somewhat outdated but no less poignant examination of a Chinese immigrant and the problems faced by him and his family in the United States.

I'm Going To Be the Lion's Head. **Xerox Films, 1972.**

In San Francisco's Chinatown, a Chinese American boy hopes for a role in the lion dance in the Chinese New Year celebration.

Jade Snow Wong. **Films, Inc., 1976.**

Wong, an author and ceramic artist, pursued her own career goals rather than taking over her family's sewing factory. This dramatized biography depicts the tension between her personal goals and her Chinese heritage.

The Joy Luck Club, **1993. Directed by Wayne Wang.**

The screen version of Amy Tan's critically acclaimed novel. Ming Na Wen is part of a strong ensemble cast in this multigenerational tale of the immigrant experience and the bond between mothers and daughters. For mature audiences.

Living Music for Golden Mountains. **University of California Extension Media Center, 1981.**

Leo Lew, a musician from southern China, tells the story of his immigration to the United States and his commitment to teaching Cantonese music to future generations of Chinese Americans.

Maxine Hong Kingston Talks About Her Writing. KQED San Francisco, 1990.

Maxine Hong Kingston wrote *The Woman Warrior*, a novel about a Chinese American woman haunted by ghosts of her childhood and by the historical figure Hua Mu-ban, a woman of the Sui Dynasty who disguised herself as a man in order to take her father's place in the military.

My Family Business. Films Inc., 1974.

In the second segment of this film, Mei Ling Lee describes her work as a waitress in her parents' New Jersey restaurant.

Sewing Woman. Picture Start, 1982.

This film is based on the life of the filmmaker's mother, Zem Ping Dong, and is drawn from oral history. Dong immigrated to the United States from China and worked in American garment factories for over thirty years. Married at age thirteen in China, she immigrated to the United States as a war bride.

Slaying the Dragon. National Asian American Telecommunications Association, 1990.

This film discusses how Asian women are portrayed in American films and television.

The Trouble with Chinatown. Films Inc., 1970.

An examination of the social and educational structure of Chinatown in New York City. Interviews with Chinese Americans illuminate reasons for Chinatown's current problems, including increased immigration and a growing generation gap.

The Wedding Banquet, 1993. Directed by Ang Lee.

A Chinese American businessman marries a beautiful Chinese artist to help her get her green card. Unexpectedly, his parents come in from Taiwan for the wedding, and he must hide the fact that the wedding is a sham. For mature audiences.

CHINESE AMERICAN LITERATURE

Cheung, King-Kok. *Asian-American Literature: An Annotated Bibliography*. New York: Modern Language Association, 1988.

Bibliographies can be extremely useful for finding resources in a specific subject area. This bibliography includes brief descriptions of each work cited.

Kim, Elaine. *Asian American Literature: An Introduction to the Writings and Their Social Context*. Philadelphia: Temple University Press, 1982.

This book will help you to think about the social context in which Chinese American and other Asian American literatures were written. A work of fiction often reveals much about the author's own perspectives and experiences.

Lim, Shirley G., and Amy Ling. *Reading the Literatures of Asian America*. Philadelphia: Temple University Press, 1992.

Lim and Ling discuss important factors and themes to consider when reading the works of Asian American writers.

Ling, Amy. *Between Worlds: Women Writers of Chinese Ancestry*. New York: Pergamon, 1990.

Chinese American women writers, such as Amy Tan and Maxine Hong Kingston, have gained popularity among Americans of all ethnicities. Ling looks at the special challenges faced by Chinese American women writers and the unique strengths they bring to their work.

Peck, David R. *American Ethnic Literatures: Native American, African American, Chicano/Latino, and Asian American Writers and Their Backgrounds: An Annotated Bibliography.* **Pasadena, CA: Salem, 1992.**

This is another useful bibliography for researching works by Asian American writers and finding information that has been written about them.

Wong, Sau-ling C. *Reading Asian American Literature: From Necessity to Extravagance.* **Princeton, NJ: Princeton University Press, 1993.**

Wong discusses prevalent themes in Asian American literature.

Chapter 3
Social Structure and Genealogy in Chinese History

There are many ways to interpret the past. For your own genealogical study, you may not know how to begin. Perhaps you feel bombarded by information. Try to keep an open mind. Do not rush to hasty conclusions. Giving yourself time will enable you to enrich your project. Reading difficult books is both challenging and rewarding.

It is important to focus on one source of information at a time. Historical resources can be overwhelming. Being too ambitious will lead only to frustration. Not only does it take time to find the exact answer to a query, but in gathering vast amounts of information, you may lose sight of your path. It is fine to feel a bit lost.

Think of genealogy as a tapestry. No matter which threads you pull, they are all part of the same fabric.

Social Structure in Ancient China

Before your ancestors immigrated to the United States, they lived in an entirely different world, a world of close kinship ties and strict concepts of social hierarchy. Families were members of clans that were the very fabric of life in ancient China, and an exacting code of social hierarchy was enforced by philosophical and political forces.

The Chinese philosopher Confucius (551–479 BC) maintained that there was a strict hierarchy of relations among people, depending on their stations in life and also their seniority. Imperial families were of the highest ranks, while common farmers and laborers were of the lowest. This social structure probably influenced the development of Chinese genealogy, which was an important tool for proving close-ness to high-ranking families and entitlement to privileges associated with those families. As in all cultures, the social elite had a vested interest in documenting the scope of its influence.

Imperial Family Structure

The best documented Chinese families are, not surprisingly, imperial families. During the Chou Dynasty (c. 1027–256 BC), Chinese emperors kept many wives and concubines, and an emperor could have many offspring. Only the eldest son of a legal wife, however, could succeed to the throne. The remaining sons were all considered feudal princes (*zhu hou*) and were lumped together into one clan. Feudal princes each had their own fiefdoms and imitated the inheritance patterns of the imperial family. Thus, only the eldest son of a *zhu hou*'s legal wife could retain the hereditary title of *zhu hou*. Not every *zhu hou* is a member of the royal clan.

The further removed from the emperor, the lower the social standing. Descendants beyond the fifth generation were considered commoners and were excluded from Confucian funerary rites. During the Chou Dynasty, members of the imperial family had to marry within the same surname in order to preserve their link to the royal bloodline. In this kind of household, the status of the eldest legal son, or *di zhang zhi*, was extremely high. The sons of the concubines held a lower social rank (although there are examples of plots by concubines to put their sons on the throne).

Chinese Clan Formation

Some scholars believe that Chinese clans developed from economic relationships. In general, clan structures have been stronger in southern China than in northern China. The economy in southern China depends on rice. In order to grow rice, one needs to maximize labor and mobilize a tremendous amount of capital. Economic historians believe that when settlers first advanced into southern China, they

The Chinese philosopher Confucius (551–479 BC) believed that there are strict hierarchies among people. This belief may have influenced the development of Chinese genealogy, as the elite sought to document its position of power.

banded together into work teams. These work teams were organized by kin group. The larger the kinship group, the greater the ability to mobilize the necessary capital.

It was in everyone's best interest to emphasize kinship ties and to widen the scope of kinship groups. The larger and more inclusive the clan, the larger and more productive the work team.

The *Zupu*: A Chinese Genealogy

The Chinese have been developing genealogical methods for centuries. Chinese genealogies were originally compiled for the imperial families and the social elite by the literati, Chinese society's educated class. There was even a special branch of the imperial bureaucracy dedicated exclusively to genealogical compilation. However, one must approach these genealogies with a critical eye. For instance, the Chinese equivalent of a Western genealogy, called a *zupu* or clan register, depicts a clan in the way its members wish to be perceived. (The *zupu* is discussed in more detail in chapter 5.) Persons who were not accepted by the clan, for whatever reason, may or may not have had their names recorded in the *zupu*.

The *zupu* was made up of the *pu*, or genealogy, and the *die*, or biographical sketch. A *pu* was a table of parallel columns dividing generations. Lines between the parallel columns were used to link individuals across generations. A *die* contained a brief narrative of a man's vital statistics.

Another important aspect of the *zupu* is that it was compiled and written by men, for men. If women were mentioned at all, they were usually the wives of prominent men. Women might also be praised as examples for others to follow if they displayed exemplary behavior in accordance with Confucian ideals.

A genealogy in ancient China was a way of accounting for noteworthy clan members. It was another way of saying, "We have many prominent people in our group. We are powerful."

Literati—the educated elite of Chinese society—were the original compilers of traditional Chinese genealogies.

Watersheds in Chinese Genealogical Compilation

Compilations of Chinese genealogies have undergone vast transformations throughout history. Depending upon social conditions, genealogies have changed to fit the times. Before the T'ang dynasty (618–907 AD), genealogies documented only relationships among the elite. However, social and political change during the T'ang dynasty paved the way during the Sung dynasty (960–1279 AD) for families of lower status to begin compiling their own genealogies.

The Ch'ing dynasty (1644–1912 AD), established by the Manchu ethnic minority, placed a ban called *pu jin* on genealogical compilation, primarily in the highly educated Jiangzhe region of China. However, the ban could not be strictly enforced, and in some regions, families still maintained and compiled genealogies. Tragically, in the twentieth century, as a result of Communist rule in China and the Cultural Revolution of the 1960s, many documents including *zupus* were destroyed forever.

Genealogical Compilation Throughout Chinese History

The genealogies of the Chou Dynasty (c.1027–256 BC) basically excluded anyone outside the direct lineage of either the imperial family or palace ministers. Some historians believe that during the Han Dynasty (202 BC–220 AD), belonging to a clan and possessing a surname as well as a lineage name brought prestige. Ancestral rites were reserved for those who were part of an officially recognized lineage.

During the Wei (220 AD–265 AD) and Chin (265–420 AD) dynasties, genealogies recorded social status. In addition to a hierarchy of individuals, there was also a ranking among clans. Most genealogies were confined to the so-called hundred households, or *bai jia*. The *bai jia* were the most common surnames of ancient times.

Many of the families that were once prominent lost their foothold during the T'ang Dynasty (618–907 AD). Corresponding to social changes during the T'ang were also changes in China's political structure. By the end of the T'ang, the so-called nine ranks of officialdom—the organizational hierarchy of the Chinese government—were obliterated.

During the Sung Dynasty (960–1279 AD), genealogies were compiled less for the sake of the state, and more to maintain the ancestral traditions of individual families. No longer were genealogies confined to the *bai jia*. Those previously considered commoners began to compile genealogies.

The Ch'ing Dynasty (1644–1912 AD) was another major turning point in genealogical compilation. The Ch'ing Dynasty was established by the Manchu, who were considered outsiders by the dominant Han people. The Manchu not only feared a Han resistance, but also that their own people might become assimilated. Many imperial court scholars criticized the Ch'ing regime, writing histories that were considered politically threatening. Other court scholars expressed their frustration in the form of poetry.

Because of this, certain policies were developed to control the Han people. One of these policies was the ban on genealogies (*pu jin*). If genealogies created a stronger sense of kinship ties among certain clans, one can imagine the threat this must have posed to the imperial family. The Ch'ing rulers saw the Jiangzhe literati as a threat because they were erecting shrines. Building ancestral shrines not only symbolized group cohesion but was also an indicator of wealth. It was hoped that the banning of genealogies would curtail shrine building.

After 1776, the fortieth year of the reign of Ch'ien-lung, a famous Ch'ing emperor, many Ch'ing officials slackened their enforcement of the ban. In spite of this, the Ch'ing ban left its mark on Chinese genealogies.

After the Ch'ing Dynasty, which officially ended in 1912, China fell into a period of political turmoil. The Communist Revolution and the Cultural Revolution led by Mao Zedong ushered in a new philosophy regarding social structure. Mao was determined to have a classless society and launched a campaign called the Cultural Revolution in the 1960s which sought to rid China of the educated elite. Many schools were closed, educated Chinese such as the literati were persecuted and driven from the country, and most traditional forms of literacy and art were discouraged. The social and political instability of this modern era forever transformed the way people viewed themselves. The power of large clans and emperors no longer held much sway.

The Impact of History on Your Search

The interesting aspect of tracing your family roots throughout Chinese history is that information about your family will have been affected by historical trends. If you are trying to find out about a relative alive during the 1950s or 1960s, traditional clan records might not be the best resource. The Communists, still in power as of this writing, deplored much of Chinese tradition, discouraged the maintenance of clan records, and even destroyed many *zupu*s. If you want to trace your roots even farther back in Chinese history and you suspect that your family was not of the elite class, the most fruitful approach to research might focus on the Sung Dynasty and the periods following. If you find through research that your family was of the elite, then a more thorough examination of genealogies in earlier time periods may also pay off.

Genealogies in the Age of Individualism

Your relatives immigrated to the United States for a reason. Perhaps they came here as contract laborers or as students, perhaps they came in search of a higher standard of living or to avoid living under a particular political regime. Immigration has probably transformed their lives, and by extension yours.

Despite research into the history of China, its social structures, and your genealogical history, you may still feel far removed from the world of your ancestors. If this is the case, think instead about the meaning of genealogy for yourself. You are probably not writing a genealogy to glorify your clan; you are probably creating a genealogy in these modern times as a self-fulfilling endeavor.

You know that you are a worthy individual in your own right. Your genealogy may one day become a valued family treasure. Save family pictures. Start keeping a diary. You have the chance to make a mark in history, modest though it may be. By creating a genealogy, you will also be carrying on an ancient Chinese tradition.

Resources

LINEAGE AND FAMILY

Chen Chihing. *Chin 500 nien lai Fuchien ti chia tsu she hui yu wen hua (500 Years of Lineage, Society, and Culture in Fujian China).* **Shanghai: Hsin hua shu tien, 1990.**

> Chinese lineages were specific to certain regions in China. If your relatives came from Fujian, China, this book will help you understand the clans from this province and how they were an outgrowth of agricultural communities. Many of the first Chinese immigrants to the United States were from Fujian.

Croll, Elisabeth; Davin, Delia; and Kane, Penny, eds. *China's One-Child Family Policy.* **Basingstoke, Hampshire, U.K.: Macmillan, 1985.**

> In order to control population growth, China's Communist government instituted a one-child policy that began during the 1970s. Families were given food rations based upon a three-person limit. This policy completely transformed the traditional notion of the large Chinese family. This book provides a thorough examination of the one-child policy.

Eberhard, Wolfram. "Chinese Genealogy as a Source for the Study of Chinese Society," in Palmer, Spencer J. *Studies in Asian Genealogy.* **Provo, UT: Brigham Young University Press, 1972.**

> This article gives detailed information about Chinese names. As you begin to locate your ancestors, keep in mind that a person could have formal, diminutive, or

affectionate names. Read this book to prepare for some of the pitfalls associated with Chinese genealogical work.

Freedman, Maurice. *Chinese Lineage and Society: Fukien and Kwangtung*. New York: Humanities Press, 1966.

In order to sustain the rice economy, Chinese clans have always been stronger in southern China than in northern China. This does not mean that if your relatives came from northern China you will be without any materials to do your research. However, keep in mind that the more prominent a clan, the greater your chances are for locating a *zupu*.

————, ed. *Family and Kinship in Chinese Society*. Stanford, CA: Stanford University Press, 1970.

Most of the articles contained in this reference have been presented at academic conferences. Although scholarly writings can be dry, the articles will give you a basis for starting your research. This book has been used by colleges as a standard reference for understanding the Chinese family.

Levy, Marion J. *The Family Revolution in Modern China*. New York: Octagon Books, 1963.

After 1949, when the Communist regime gained control of China, there were many changes in the conception of family to prepare for the restructured agricultural society.

Liu, Hui-chen. *The Traditional Chinese Clan Rules*. Locust Valley, NY: published for the Association of Asian Studies, 1959.

An in-depth analysis of Chinese clan rules. Do you ever wonder what it would be like to live by the rules of a clan or tribe? Every clan member's behavior was regulated by strict rules. Clan members had to follow certain rules about whom they could marry. Men might be required to participate in ancestral rites. These stringent rules contributed to social cohesion and stability, though they might seem cumbersome to us today.

Whyte, Martin King. *Urban Life in Contemporary China*. Chicago: University of Chicago Press, 1984.

What is the quality of life for most urban families in China? This book addresses how the urban economy affects the Chinese family. What kind of family did your ancestors come from? If they were city dwellers, this book might be especially interesting to you.

Chapter 4
Starting Your Search in the United States

Not all research on Chinese ancestry is limited to China. The U.S. government has been keeping records of its citizens and visitors for nearly two centuries. Chinese people who gave birth in U.S. hospitals, married here, served in the military, worked for the government, attended U.S. schools, or died here left behind official documents that are of great value to a genealogist. Chinese Americans who were born here or were naturalized as citizens leave an even clearer path for future generations of genealogists to follow.

Vital Records

In genealogy, nothing is considered a fact until it has been proved with an official record. The most trusted records in the United States are birth, marriage, and death certificates. These fall into the category of vital records. You may be told "facts" about your ancestors, or even read them in some official publication such as the census. But until they have been verified with a vital document, they are only conjecture.

Some of these vital records may be as close at hand as your relatives' homes. Before you write or visit any archives, you should do a thorough search for records in your family's possession. Ask for permission to hunt through boxes, files, or wherever your family may store important documents. Families often keep copies or originals of vital records. Whatever you are unable to find, ask your relatives about. Perhaps you can find an uncle's death certificate but not his birth certificate. Ask his widow, your aunt, whether he was born in the United States. If so, does she know the state and county? Most vital records in the United States are archived in the courthouse of the county where the event took place.

With few exceptions, any event that could affect ownership of real property (land and its attachments) is recorded
as a matter of public record by the county. Birth and death
certificates are recorded for this purpose, as are marriage
certificates, deeds, and mortgages. Name changes are often
recorded as well. You may not be able to visit every county
courthouse from which you need information. At your local
public library, ask a librarian to help you find the addresses
for U.S. courthouses. You will need to write letters asking
for exactly the information you need, including the relative's
name, the event for which you need a record, and the ap-
proximate date. You may be sent an official form for requesting a record, and there may be a fee charged for
research and photocopying. Consult Thomas J. Kemp's
International Vital Records Handbook for information on
obtaining vital records from every county, state, and country.
Kemp's book even includes standard forms requesting vital
records; you only need to fill them out and send them to the
address provided.

County records of transactions involving land are usually
stored in the office of the county recorder. They are ordered
in an index either chronologically or by the legal description
(exact location) of the property affected, not usually by the
individual's name. This makes finding information about
particular individuals a time-consuming but interesting
project. If you know that your relatives bought or sold land
in a particular area, it is probably worth the effort to seek
out land records.

You should begin your research from the most recent date
possible and work backward through time. Each index item
corresponds with a document that was filed in that county.
In the index, you will find names of *Grantor*(s) (person,
persons, or entity which holds title to the property prior to
execution of the document), *Grantee*(s) (person, persons, or
entity which will hold title to the property after execution of
the document), a property description, and information
about where the document is stored. A review of that docu-

ment will often refer to other documents, names, or proper-
ties. Until recently, the indexes were recorded manually in
ledgers. Be sure to take a magnifying glass. You may need it
to decipher a second-generation photocopy of an index
written 112 years ago.

If you know only the name of the relative who died in a
particular county, start at the cemetery. Cemeteries can be
very valuable tools to a researcher. If you know nothing
more than the fact that your forebears once lived in the area,
you may find yourself making notes about every Chinese
name you find. From an ancestor's gravestone, you should
be able to obtain dates of birth and death. Once you have a
date to start with, visit the county recorder's office and begin
your document search.

If you know a name and date or year of a birth, death, or
marriage, make a list of the name or names that you expect
to find in the courthouse records. Ask for the index for that
time period and start reading. Once you find a name that
you are searching for, you will need to review the referenced
document. Remember, not everybody with the same surname is related.

Make sure that you have found the right individual. If you
have found a birth record, add the names of the child and
parents to your list and go back to the index. If you have
found a death record, amend your list and return to the
index to look for documents such as deeds or wills that were
recorded near the death date. If you have found a deed or
will, make a copy of it and return to the index.

Documents that transfer property ownership (such as
deeds and wills) will give you the date of the transfer,
name(s) of the grantor(s) and grantee(s), a legal description
of the property, and a reference to the last vesting document
of that transferred title. A vesting document is any recorded
document that officially transfers property ownership or title.
Marriage records will give you the names of both the bride
and the groom. Even if a woman decides to take her husband's surname after the marriage, she signs the marriage

certificate in her maiden name. You may also find that marriage records offer ages, residences, and religious affiliations. Common-law marriages (couples who had no official marriage ceremony) may be indicated in deeds or tax records. A vital record may give you information not just about a specific event, but also about other people, places, or dates that will lead you further along a family line.

Chinese Names

Surnames first developed in China in 2852 BC when it was decreed by the emperor that all families should choose a name from the *Po-Chia-Hsing*, a sacred poem. Because the poem had so few characters, today there are only about sixty common Chinese surnames. Unlike some other ethnic groups, Chinese immigrants to the United States did not generally Americanize their surnames. This is probably due to the importance of family and ancestral ties in Chinese culture and the fact that Chinese names are usually short and easy to pronounce. This is good news for many Chinese American genealogists, who will not have the same problem faced by some Americans whose family names were changed to sound more "American." Of course, if your surname was spelled differently or incorrectly by immigration officials, census takers, hospitals, or other records sources, this may cause some problems, so be aware of the possibility that different variations of your name may exist. This can complicate your search.

You should know about Chinese naming conventions. A Chinese name basically consists of a surname and a given name. Romanized Chinese names (names that have been written in the Roman alphabet) present a problem. You can romanize a Chinese name in a variety of ways, but you cannot necessarily determine the character that corresponds to the name by looking at the English spelling. Your parents or other relatives should be able to help you find the Chinese character that represents your surname.

Sometimes the very way a Chinese name is romanized can

give clues about the region in China a family comes from. For instance, Moy, Yee, and Tom are names of Cantonese origin.

Another complication is the variety of Chinese dialects. The exact same Chinese character could be pronounced differently by Chinese depending on their region of origin. Thus the Chinese surname Lin is pronounced "Lin" by a northern Chinese and "Lum" by a southern Chinese. If you were doing a comprehensive search of records for the Lin family, you would need to consider all possible spellings of the character *lin* as it is rendered into English.

Unlike European names, Chinese surnames precede given names. Many people, particularly from elite families, used nicknames of sorts. Depending upon the level of formality, a different name would be applied. Some characters in Chinese names actually represent ancient titles. These are all issues to keep in mind as you research your family history.

Creating a Genealogy

Your identity as a Chinese American puts you in an interesting position. How can your genealogy best reflect who you are? Should you create a genealogy that resembles a traditional Chinese genealogy? Or should you use family group sheets and pedigree charts that were originally created for European American genealogies? The decision is your own. There is nothing to stop you from integrating both approaches.

Family group sheets and pedigree charts are forms for a standard genealogy. A family group sheet shows nuclear family units consisting of a married or single head of household and offspring. Look at the family group sheet on page 78. Write down the names, dates of birth, and places of birth for your parents, yourself, and your siblings. If your parents have divorced and remarried, make a separate family group sheet for their family unit. The family group sheet is the basis for your pedigree chart. Once you complete family group sheets for many generations, you can link them together chronologically. Examine the pedigree chart on page

79. The pedigree chart shows information on different generations in a family line. Each member of a family is assigned a number, and keeps this number on additional charts. You will be number one on the pedigree chart; the chart then moves backward in time (to the right on the page) as increasing numbers show preceding generations.

The *zupu* is the traditional format for a Chinese genealogy. Because you are Chinese American, you might want to consider incorporating some elements of a *zupu* into your genealogy. The *zupu* format has limitations, such as the lack of information about female family members. You may feel that your grandmother, mother, sister, and other female relatives deserve more than a traditional Chinese *zupu* offers them. See chapter 5 for more information on the *zupu* format.

In your pedigree chart, you may want to utilize the Chinese technique of appending more information about each individual as you find it. Each appended piece of information that pertains to a family member should be attached in numerical order and correspond to the number listed on the pedigree chart.

Reaching the Shores

Vital records or word of mouth from your relatives can lead you to the place where your ancestors first took up residence in the United States. The next step is to find the port where they landed, also known as the port of entry. The more recent the landing was, the more likely that records of your ancestor's arrival still exist.

The best place to begin is at the harbor nearest the location where your ancestor was first recorded as living. The first place of residence was likely also the port of entry. The county courthouse or local maritime museum may be able to show you passenger lists for the year in which your ancestor arrived.

This process may not be so straightforward if you have traced your ancestor to an inland county. In that case, you may need to rely on private letters, diaries, and newspaper

FAMILY GROUP WORK SHEET #_____

HUSBAND, Name: WIFE, Name:
Birth: Place: Birth: Place:
Death: Place: Death: Place:
Burial: Place: Burial: Place:
Father: Father:
Mother: Mother:
Occupation: Occupation:
Notes: Notes:

Name	Date & Place of Birth	Date & Place of Marriage	Date & Place of Death	Married to	Date & Place of Birth Death

clippings to help you figure out the port of entry. You may also find it helpful to write to the Immigration and Naturalization Service, Washington, DC 20536, for information on relatives who came to this country after 1906. The Church of Jesus Christ of Latter-day Saints Family History Library in Salt Lake City, Utah, and regional Family History Centers, which will be discussed in more detail later in this chapter, have copies of ship passenger lists. If you are not

Pedigree Chart

Name of Compiler _____

Address _____

City, State _____

Date _____

Person No.1 on this chart is the same person as No.____ on chart No.____.

Chart No.____

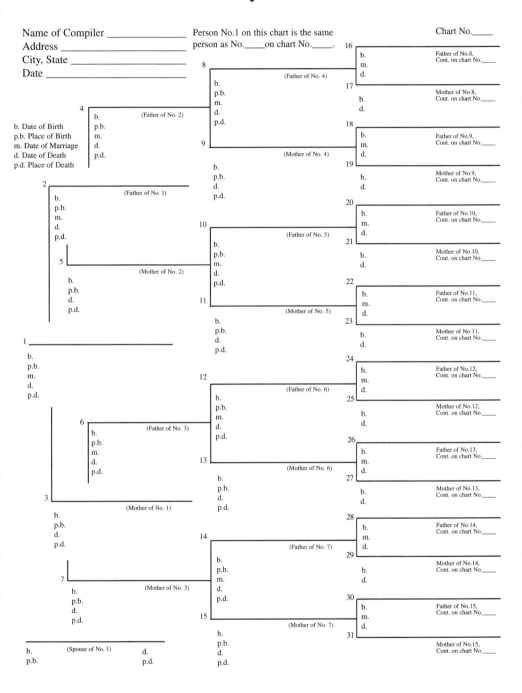

8 (Father of No. 4)
b.
p.b.
m.
d.
p.d.

4 (Father of No. 2)
b.
p.b.
m.
d.
p.d.

b. Date of Birth
p.b. Place of Birth
m. Date of Marriage
d. Date of Death
p.d. Place of Death

9 (Mother of No. 4)
b.
p.b.
d.
p.d.

2 (Father of No. 1)
b.
p.b.
m.
d.
p.d.

5 (Mother of No. 2)
b.
p.b.
d.
p.d.

10 (Father of No. 5)
b.
p.b.
m.
d.
p.d.

11 (Mother of No. 5)
b.
p.b.
d.
p.d.

1 _____
b.
p.b.
m.
d.
p.d.

6 (Father of No. 3)
b.
p.b.
m.
d.
p.d.

12 (Father of No. 6)
b.
p.b.
m.
d.
p.d.

13 (Mother of No. 6)
b.
p.b.
d.
p.d.

3 (Mother of No. 1)
b.
p.b.
d.
p.d.

7 (Mother of No. 3)
b.
p.b.
d.
p.d.

14 (Father of No. 7)
b.
p.b.
m.
d.
p.d.

15 (Mother of No. 7)
b.
p.b.
d.
p.d.

(Spouse of No. 1)
b.
p.b.
d.
p.d.

16 Father of No.8,
Cont. on chart No.____
b.
m.
d.

17 Mother of No.8,
Cont. on chart No.____
b.
d.

18 Father of No.9,
Cont. on chart No.____
b.
m.
d.

19 Mother of No.9,
Cont. on chart No.____
b.
d.

20 Father of No.10,
Cont. on chart No.____
b.
m.
d.

21 Mother of No.10,
Cont. on chart No.____
b.
d.

22 Father of No.11,
Cont. on chart No.____
b.
m.
d.

23 Mother of No.11,
Cont. on chart No.____
b.
d.

24 Father of No.12,
Cont. on chart No.____
b.
m.
d.

25 Mother of No.12,
Cont. on chart No.____
b.
d.

26 Father of No.13,
Cont. on chart No.____
b.
m.
d.

27 Mother of No.13,
Cont. on chart No.____
b.
d.

28 Father of No.14,
Cont. on chart No.____
b.
m.
d.

29 Mother of No.14,
Cont. on chart No.____
b.
d.

30 Father of No.15,
Cont. on chart No.____
b.
m.
d.

31 Mother of No.15,
Cont. on chart No.____
b.
d.

sure of your ancestors' exact port of entry, check the lists for
San Francisco and Honolulu first; these were common
points of entry for Chinese immigrants.

Just as your immigrant ancestors probably suffered culture
shock in the United States, you too will depart from familiar
ground if you choose to explore further. Your journey back
in time to China will involve dedication and perseverance.

Locating Chinese Roots

At a reference library you will have access to a wide variety
of resources. Your first move should be to determine
whether any family histories have already been written about
the family line that you are researching. It is possible that a
great deal of work has been done for you already. A librarian
can help you use the holdings catalog to see whether their
library has any information on your family. She or he can
direct you to indexes of both published and unpublished
manuscripts on family history. The Online Computer Library Center (OCLC) will show which libraries hold books
that might be of use to you. You may be able to order these
materials through interlibrary loan, a service that is often free
to library patrons. Ask your librarian. He or she will be
happy to help you.

If you are not lucky enough to find prepared family history
manuscripts, following the steps below will lead you to many
more facts about your family tree.

Choose a format for your Chinese American genealogy.
Follow the steps below to gather information. Go to your
local library and see if the reference librarian can help you.

1) Talk to relatives and friends and neighbors of your
relatives. Chinese people, even today, often live in tightly
knit communities. Older members of the community may be
excellent resources.

2) Gather together scrapbooks, photos, letters, and keep-
sakes of your immediate family. Sometimes our grandparents
have kept things they have since forgotten about. My grandfather kept an old teakwood box in his study that was clearly
forgotten. This box was full of pictures of my long deceased

grandmother and many other relatives, including a photo of my own mother when she was eight years old.

3) Check for the various names that ancestors could have been known by. For example, a deceased Chinese Hawaiian American named Wong Aloiau was also known as Loiau, Ah Loy Yau, and Wong Young Hong (an honorific name). The honorific name was the one that appeared on his tombstone. Verify Chinese surnames (the actual Chinese characters), using tombstones or letters addressed to your relatives.

4) Check the U.S. Census. Since 1790 the U.S. government has taken a population census every ten years. These documents can be like treasure maps to genealogists. Each census is kept confidential until most of the people listed in it have died. Recently, the 1920 census was made public for the first time. In a genealogical search, it is best to begin with the most recent census and work your way back. That way, you can fill in the picture of where your ancestors lived and moved to, where they were born, and then move on to the same information about their parents. Keep in mind that Chinese living in the United States were listed for the first time in the 1870 census.

The National Archives is the official repository for the U.S. Census. Unfortunately, many of the records before 1890 were destroyed in a fire. The more recent censuses and what remains of the previous censuses are available on microfiche. Copies are held at many large research libraries. Begin with the census index for the state in which your ancestor lived. Look up your ancestor by surname and find out the county census in which your ancestor's complete entry appears, as well as the page and line number. With this information you can write to the National Archives and order a photocopy of the exact page of the county census you need (National Archives General Reference Branch, Washington, DC 20408). Family members are listed under the male head of household. The census will provide you with year of birth, year of arrival from China, occupation, English proficiency (whether the head of household could read, write, or speak English), name of spouse, and names

Documents such as the Certificate of Residence, an example of which is shown above, can be useful in piecing together the history of your immigrant ancestors. In 1892, the year this certificate was issued, the Chinese Exclusion Act of 1882 had been extended. The act excluded Chinese laborers but allowed merchants, students, teachers, diplomats, and travelers to enter the United States under certain conditions.

and birthdates of children. Sometimes, other people living in the same house were also recorded.

5) Apply to receive copies of death certificates at the appropriate department of health in the area where your ancestor lived. The death certificate will provide names of parents. This can take you back one generation. It may lead you directly to Chinese soil if the birthplaces of the parents are provided.

6) Check tombstones. Sometimes tombstones provide information about place of origin in China (province and district). They can also provide dates of birth and death.

7) Family History Library. The world's largest genealogy library is in Utah. It is run by the Church of Jesus Christ of Latter-day Saints (LDS), also called the Mormons. Although you may not be able to visit Salt Lake City to do research at

this remarkable facility, LDS is working hard to make their
collection available to family historians everywhere. Write to
them for a list of their regional branches, called Family
History Centers, where you will find helpful volunteers to
steer you in the right direction on your search. You might
also check your local telephone directory to locate a Family
History Center. (Family History Library, 35 North West
Temple Street, Salt Lake City, UT 84150.)

One of LDS's most useful databases is the International
Genealogy Index (IGI). This database includes information
from vital records, censuses, published family histories,
historical gazetteers, and atlases. These records are indexed
by surname and cover 150 million individuals who died
between 1500 and 1875. There is no other database like
the IGI.

Many of the LDS databases are becoming available on
CD-ROM, so they are available for library and home purchase.
LDS also offers a search register, where family historians can
sign up to exchange information on certain surnames.

8) Military records. Thousands of Chinese American men
and women have served in the U.S. armed forces. To receive forms for requesting information about an ancestor in
the U.S. military, write to Military Personnel Records, 9700
Page Boulevard, St. Louis, MO 63132.

9) Soundex. Beginning with the 1880 U.S. Census, many
census records have been indexed using the Soundex coding
system, which sorts names by their sounds. Soundex is
usually available on microfilm of the original card file, and
its value is enormous, especially when you don't know where
a particular family lived. The film is arranged by state, then
alphabetically by the first letter of the surname, then chronologically by Soundex code (e.g. number 1 = b, p, f, v; 5 =
m, n, etc). Chinese names may be coded under the first
word of the name or the name that appears last even though
this may not be the actual surname. Census takers may not
have been aware of the Chinese practice of placing the surname before the given (first) name. To find a household,
you may have to check various possibilities.

Chinese Americans have served in many U.S. wars, which makes it likely that information about some of your ancestors can be found in U.S. military records. This Chinese American soldier served in World War I.

Tracing Your Roots If You Are Adopted

If you are an adopted Chinese American, you have probably wondered about your family history. You can explore two worlds: that of your adoptive family or that of your birth parents. The concept of family is what you make of it. If you were adopted by European Americans, you are lucky to be truly bicultural. It is perfectly normal to wonder who your natural parents are. Perhaps when you arise every morning and look in the mirror, you examine your physical features. You wonder what your birth parents looked like. Were they Chinese Americans? Were you born of immigrant Chinese parents?

You may have asked many times about your roots because you are clearly of a different ethnicity than your adoptive family. How might you get information about your birth parents? Legal action is required if you are a minor. Many adoption records are sealed to protect the identity of birth parents.

Once you reach eighteen years of age, you may be able to examine legally sealed adoption records. Many sensitive issues surround custody. To avoid hurt feelings, talk openly with your adoptive parents about your wishes. It is possible that your birth parents may not be in a position to meet you. Consider all these things before you move ahead with your plans.

Fortunately, genealogy does not require having to meet your birth parents. As we have emphasized throughout this volume, you are the creator of your genealogy. When you reach the age of eighteen, although you are legally entitled to know about them, your search for your birth parents may not be easy.

Instead, you may want to research the history of your adoptive family. After all, you are part of their family now; what better way to celebrate your role in it. Remember that there are others like you. Adoption support groups in your local area are listed in the phone book. These groups might be able to point you in the right direction. Adoption registers match up adoptees and birth parents who are seeking each other.

As an adopted Chinese American, nothing should stop you from learning about your own heritage. If you feel strongly about identifying with Chinese Americans as a group, you will find plenty of company. There are many things you can do to learn about your Chinese American identity.

If you are still interested in finding out more about your birth parents, consider these steps:

- Ask your adoptive parents if they know anything about your birth parents. Your adoptive parents might be willing to share a great deal with you. You may already know how your adoption came about. Many U.S. diplomats or foreign service officers who travel abroad have adopted children from the places where they were stationed. Sometimes war, poverty, or other hardships necessitate the separation of children from their birth parents. In cases such as these, your adoptive parents may relate interesting stories about your past as well as their own. Perhaps you can write these stories down and append them to your genealogical project.

- Read about China and Chinese Americans. As you read, keep a notebook handy. Something poignant may suddenly strike you. A clue from what you know to be true about your past may link up with something concrete in your life now.

Adopted or not, we all have limited knowledge about our origins. The culture we belong to is defined by our environment. You can belong to American culture without being a Caucasian person. One of my Chinese American friends found that he felt far more comfortable in the United States than in Asia because of social expectations. After all, he "looked" Chinese, so why was he acting so "American"? Unfortunately, many people judge us by the way we look instead of who we are. Because you have the chance to understand both Chinese and American culture, you will be all the less apt to prejudge others. You should be proud of your bicultural heritage.

Genealogy on the Internet

As your search leads you through Chinese history and records, remind yourself also to explore the many electronic resources that are now available. You would be hard pressed to find a college or university that does not have a computerized library catalog. You will find that institutions specifically geared toward Chinese or Asian studies often have their own computerized indexes, databases, and reference materials that can be made available to you. Although the technology surrounding computers, networks, and information handling is constantly evolving, we hope to introduce you to some avenues of research that until recently were simply not available.

Computers allow us to store and retrieve quickly large amounts of information. Most of the computerized research tools that you will encounter will be in the form of databases. A database is a program that allows the computer to manage vast amounts of information that is identical in structure but varying in content. For example, a name and address list in a computer will have many records containing the same type of information, but the data contained in each record will be different. Most libraries, public and private, have databases that can be searched for information relating to just about any topic.

Some databases allow you to search via category. You might find information about Chinese immigration by selecting the categories Asian-Chinese-Genealogy-Immigration. Other databases operate by matching words and phrases. This kind of database requires that you supply search information and criteria. Remember, computers are very literal. A search for the word "Chinese" would supply you with thousands of references to the word "Chinese." The computer would report any instance where it found a match, and you would be inundated with publications that contained that one word. On the other hand, searching for the phrase "Chinese men named Sven" would probably yield no matches. The combination of "Chinese Immigration" and "Chinatown" would offer far more manageable results. The more specific your search, the more accurately the information will suit your needs. A search for "Chin" will yield both "China" and "Chinese." Regardless of the type of database, you will find "Help" screens or printed instructions to guide you.

Since the early 1970s, government and academic institutions have been working together to create a worldwide computer network that allows people and computers to communicate with each other quickly and seamlessly. The result of their efforts is what we commonly call the Internet. In essence, the Internet is a global network that gives users at one site access to information stored on machines around the world. As technology advances and as the private sector recognizes the benefits of having such vast amounts of information at its disposal, the Internet grows, is refined, and becomes a richer source of information. For centuries, individuals, associations, and groups have dedicated immeasurable effort to the pursuit of historical and genealogical information. Now these disparate resources are on the Internet, making their years of research available to one another—and to you.

The size of the Internet is both its greatest strength and its greatest weakness. With literally tens of thousands of computers connected to the "net," you can easily gather information from educational, governmental, and private institutions. Because of its sheer size, however, searching the Internet is like looking for a needle in a haystack. To help handle this problem, designers of Internet software have developed special programs called "browsers." Internet browsers give you tools to help you navigate the net, view information, and download files. A browser will connect you, either through a telephone or direct line, to a server that has Internet access. Once connected to an Internet server, you will most likely see that server's home page, which is programmed to be interactive and mouse-driven. You will be offered, among various points of interest, a link to an Internet search engine.

The search engines keep lists of connected computers,

A Chinese American Photo Album

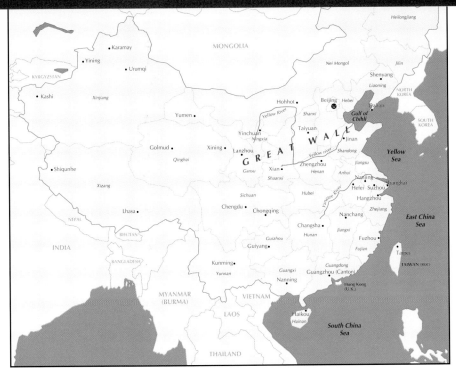

China is one of the world's oldest civilizations. A country with almost one-fifth of the global population, it boasts perhaps the most complex language in the world. Its art, literature, architecture, cuisine, politics, and history have long made it a place of popular and scholarly fascination. In the second half of the nineteenth century, economic and political instability in China created an impetus for emigration. The discovery of gold made California an attractive destination for Chinese seeking better fortunes. Jobs were plentiful in the booming American West, and work on railroads and in mines took Chinese workers from California north to the Pacific Northwest and east to the south-western states. The Chinese immigrant community did not experience the same assimilation process of other immigrant groups in American society, largely because of restrictive and racist immigration policies that prevented families from forming or reuniting. But those who did manage to come, and stay, gave back more than they received from their adopted country in the form of hard work, loyalty, and a commitment to justice. Subsequent relaxation of immigration restrictions allowed more Chinese immigrants to contribute their energy, intelligence, and skills to American society. Today, China remains one of the "top ten" countries from which immigrants arrive in the United States. While they still face obstacles, these recent immigrants have many Chinese American role models who have prospered and are leaders in every field of endeavor.

The Great Wall of China is a 1,500-mile-long fortification that runs along the country's northern and northwestern frontier, stretching from the Gulf of Chihli in the east to the Gansu Province in the west. Construction of the Great Wall was begun during the reign of Emperor Shih Huang Ti in the third century BC to bar Mongolian invaders. It was extended to its current length in the Ming Dynasty between 1368 and 1644 AD. The Great Wall is the only human-made structure on Earth visible from outer space.

Above, a man in Ritan Park, Beijing, performs his early morning tai chi chuan exercises, a ritual for millions of city dwellers. Tai chi chuan is an ancient discipline, a system of self-defense and an aid to meditation. It emphasizes slow, relaxed, circular body movements. Tai chi chuan is the most popular form of individual exercise in China.

On June 4, 1989, the Chinese Liberation Army opened fire on a group of 100,000 pro-democracy protesters who had gathered in Tiananmen Square in Beijing. The attack, which left hundreds of Chinese protesters dead and thousands more wounded, provoked international outrage. Here, Chinese American demonstrators hold signs and American flags in front of the Chinese Embassy in Washington, DC, to protest the Chinese government's violent actions in Tiananmen Square.

Chinese society has undergone dramatic changes in recent years as the government has adopted a number of economic reforms. Above, entrepreneurs seek to better their fortunes by selling souvenirs on the steps of the Yellow Crane Pagoda in Wuhan in December, 1992.

Chinese opera, a form of musical drama, was traditionally based on folktales about heroes and the supernatural. Today in China it often focuses on the heroes of the Communist Revolution or great events of China's recent past. Performers in Chinese opera commonly wear colorful costumes and bright makeup, as does this performer.

Martial artist Jackie Chan has become Asia's number one box-office star and a popular actor with American moviegoers. Above, Chinese American director Ang Lee presents Chan (right) with Asian Cinevision's Lifetime Achievement Award on February 1, 1996, in New York City. Lee himself has won critical acclaim for his films *Sense and Sensibility*, *Eat Drink Man Woman*, and *The Wedding Banquet*.

The Chinese New Year, which falls in late January or early February, is the most important of all annual Chinese festivals. Above, the city of Hong Kong celebrates the beginning of the Year of the Rat on February 21, 1996. According to the Chinese calendar, each year is represented by one of twelve different animals, following each other in rotation. The reason, Chinese legend says, is that when Buddha summoned all of the animals on Earth to him, only twelve obeyed. These twelve animals were rewarded for their loyalty to Buddha, who named a year after each one.

The Chinese New Year is celebrated by Chinese Americans across the United States. During the festival, celebrants participate in traditional family activities, such as paying homage to ancestors and eating a New Year's feast. Community celebrations often involve large parades with floats and performances, like this Dragon Dance in Chicago.

Large numbers of recent immigrants from China and Hong Kong have helped revitalize the many urban Chinatown districts in the United States. New York City's Chinatown is known for vendors selling fresh fruits, vegetables, and fish at stands such as the one shown above.

Since the early days of helping construct the Central Pacific Railroad in the 1860s, Chinese immigrant workers in the United States have frequently had to fight exploitation by their employers. In 1991, these Chinese workers in New York City demonstrated against garment shop owners. Several garment shops had gone out of business, their employees owing thousands of dollars in back pay.

The Chinese-inspired architecture of this building is typical of many structures in San Fancisco's Chinatown, home to more than 10,000 Chinese Americans.

Celebrated in China and the United States, the Dragon Boat Festival commemorates the fourth-century Chinese poet and patriot, Chu Yuan, who drowned himself in the Mi-lo River as a protest against government corruption. The subsequent search for his body in long dragon boats gave rise to the traditional Dragon Boat Festival, celebrated here on Boston's Charles River.

In 1989, seventeen-year-old Chinese American tennis player Michael Chang became the youngest player ever to win the French Open. Chang supports the creation of tennis programs for young people in Asian countries with his Stars of the Future program. He is one of the world's top-seeded players.

Born in Oakland, California, Amy Tan is the author of two best-selling novels, *The Joy Luck Club* and *The Kitchen God's Wife*. Chronicling the lives of four Chinese women and their immigration to the United States, *The Joy Luck Club* was a finalist for the National Book Award Critics Circle Award and was made into a major motion picture.

A nine-time Grammy Award-winner for classical music, cellist Yo-Yo Ma gave his first public recital at the age of five and began his studies at the Juilliard School in New York at the age of seven. Despite his constant touring and recording with some of the finest instrumentalists and orchestras in the world, Ma finds time to include educational outreach activities for American students in his busy schedule. Here, Ma (center) is seen with violinist Isaac Stern (left) and conductor Zubin Mehta at Carnegie Hall in New York.

where they are located, and what they offer. These lists are searched each time a request is made. Using the Web Crawler search engine, the search for "Chinese" located 1,495 references. The search for "genealogy" found 342 matches. The search for census returned 970 matches.

The results of an Internet search are presented to you in the form of an interactive list. Items in the list that appear to be highlighted are called hypertext links. If you select a hypertext entry, your computer will be automatically connected to the machine that contains that data listed by the search. Look for the most recent and useful sites on Chinese genealogy by searching under terms such as "China," "Chinese Americans," and "genealogy."

Your "Cybergenealogy"

Today, we are able to create documents in the Chinese language using various software applications. Your parents may own a basic Chinese word processor. When you create a family tree, you might consider keying in the names of your relatives, obtaining a printout, and using cut-and-paste to place the names in the right location. Fancier desktop applications would allow you to create a complete family tree. Aldus PageMaker, for example, has a Chinese version. Asian-language computers require additional tools to help set up a working environment.

Refer to any Chinese-English dictionary to get a complete list of romanizations. There are several ways to romanize Chinese. Your dictionary most likely uses either a system called Wade Giles, or Pinyin. You must input Chinese characters in the mode of the default setting. If your computer is set to Pinyin, for example, you must type Pinyin spellings in order to get the right menus.

Most households do not have Chinese desktop applications beyond simple word processors. You can use word processor output to give your genealogy a professional touch. The other advantage of Chinese word processing is that it facilitates language learning.

Creating actual Chinese documents is one way to gather

your work into something to be proud of. Another way to present your genealogy is completely online. The Internet has a number of discussion groups and home pages dedicated to certain surnames. In surfing the Internet, you will find that there is not much in the way of Chinese American genealogies, although there are a few examples. By contrast, many individuals of European origin have already started to present their genealogies on the Internet. Perhaps one day, you can be a leader the field of Chinese American genealogies online. The possibilities are endless.

Resources

GENEALOGY BASICS

Allaben, Frank, et al. *How to Trace and Record Your Own Ancestry*. **New York: National Historical Company, 1932.**

> Although this guide does not address Chinese genealogical issues in particular, it can stimulate your thoughts and lead you to pursue avenues not covered in this book. Everyone needs to be reminded of places to look for information. Includes an extensive bibliography.

Allen, Desmond Walls, and Billingsley, Carolyn Earle. *Beginner's Guide to Family History Research*. **Bountiful, UT: American Genealogical Lending Library, 1991.**

> A fine introduction to family history research. Includes many examples and chapters on organization, utilization of specific archives and libraries, use of census and other records, and interviews and correspondence.

————. *Social Security Applications: A Genealogical Resource*. **Bryant, AR: Research Associates, 1991.**

> U.S. Social Security records can be used for genealogical research. Legal immigrants need to apply for social security. Your Chinese American relatives may be traced using the techniques introduced in this guide.

American Genealogy: A Basic Course. **National Genealogical Society.**

> By writing to the National Genealogical Society at 4527 17th Street North, Arlington, VA 22207-2363, you can acquire a brochure about this program. It incorporates

both written and video guides and is an excellent introduction to beginning your search.

Balhuizen, Anne Ross. *Searching on Location: Planning a Research Trip.* **Salt Lake City: Ancestry, Inc., 1992.**

Good advice on how to plan for a research excursion. If you are fortunate enough to travel to China, you will want to maximize your time and efforts.

Bertaux, Daniel, and Bertaux, Thompson. *Between Generations: Family Models, Myths, and Memories.* **New York: Oxford University Press, 1993.**

This guide tells you how you can apply cross-cultural studies to genealogy. There is also a section on oral history.

Cache Genealogical Library, Logan, Utah. *Handbook for Genealogical Correspondence.* **Salt Lake City: Bookcraft, 1963.**

It might be difficult to do a Chinese American genealogy if you do not live near a large library. This guide addresses what, who, and where to write for genealogical information.

California State Archives. *Genealogical Research in the California State Archives.* **Sacramento: Office of the Secretary of State, California State Archives, 1976.**

What can you expect to find in the California State Archives that can help you in your genealogical quest? California has the largest concentration of Chinese Americans in the United States.

Clewer, Lisa Ray. *How to Find Your Own Roots.* **Studio City, CA.: The Works, 1977.**

A general guide to tracing your family genealogy and making a "living history" album.

Clifford, Karen. *Genealogy and Computers for the Complete Beginner*, rev. ed. Baltimore: Clearfield Company, 1995.

Computers can be important tools for both genealogical fact-finding and organization. Clifford explains how to get the most out of your computer.

Cooper, Kay. *Where Did You Get Those Eyes: A Guide to Discovering Your Family History.* New York: Walker & Co., 1988.

A thorough guide to researching your family history, from interviewing to researching in genealogical libraries.

Crowe, Elizabeth Powell. *Genealogy Online: Researching Your Roots.* New York: Windcrest/McGraw-Hill, 1995.

Crowe offers some advice on how to use the Internet in finding your roots.

Deseret Sunday School Union. *Adventures in Research.* Salt Lake City: Deseret Sunday School Union Board, 1943.

This guide was inspired by a genealogical training class. It emphasizes that when you feel that you have exhausted all possibilities, you need to follow your intuition.

Doane, Gilbert. *Searching for Your Ancestors: The How and Why of Genealogy.* Minneapolis: University of Minnesota Press, 1960.

Includes chapters on finding information in cemeteries, county courthouses, government agencies, family papers, and churches. Contains appendixes on locating vital statistics, census records, and bibliographies.

Dollarhide, William. *Genealogy Starter Kit.* Baltimore: Genealogical Publishing Co., 1994.

This thirty-two page booklet is packed with information and includes Dollarhide's seven-step system for conducting genealogical research. Numerous names and addresses will guide you to vital records offices and genealogical libraries and societies.

———. *Managing a Genealogical Project*, rev. ed. Baltimore: Genealogical Publishing Co., 1994.

Dollarhide has developed a unique system of organization for genealogical research, from the first steps to a final report or book. Includes a section on the use of computer software in genealogy.

Dunn, Phillip B. *A Guide to Ancestral Research in London*. Salt Lake City: P. B. Dunn, 1987.

This guide covers library and archival resources in England and the United States. The British Library has a collection of Chinese *zupu*.

Earnest, Russell D. *Grandma's Attic: Making Heirlooms Part of Your Family History*. Albuquerque, NM: R. D. Earnest Associates, 1991.

Focus on conservation and restoration as you approach family heirlooms. Chinese *zupu* are often printed on fragile paper. If your family has kept a *zupu*, this book will help you think about ways to preserve it. Often, people donate *zupu* to special collections at university libraries for safekeeping.

Everton, Walter Marion. *The Handy Book for Genealogists*. Logan, UT: Everton Publishers, 1991.

This volume includes a directory of genealogists who might be interested in providing input for your project.

Friedensohn, Doris, and Ruben, Barbara. *Generations of Women: In Search of Female Forebears*. Jersey City: Jersey City State College Women's Studies, 1984.

Friedensohn and Ruben focus on women in history. Their primary research method is the use of oral history. This book may be of value to you if you are particularly interested in collecting the memories of your older female relatives.

Greenwood, Val D. *The Researcher's Guide to American Genealogy.* **Baltimore: Genealogical Publishing Co., 1995.**

Learn the principles of genealogical research from this essential guide. Greenwood discusses types of records and their uses and provides up-to-date information on the newest methods and materials of importance to genealogists.

Hey, David. *The Oxford Guide to Family History.* **New York: Oxford University Press, 1993.**

Contains great chapters on searching government records and church registries. Also has information on the origin of particular family names.

Hilton, Suzanne. *Who Do You Think You Are? Digging for Your Family Roots.* **Philadelphia: Westminster Press, 1977.**

Although you will want to acquire more recent sources eventually, this book remains a good place to start your genealogical search. Written for young people.

Jacobson, Judy. *A Genealogist's Refresher Course.* **Baltimore: Clearfield Company, 1995.**

Jacobson shares her experiences in genealogical research, emphasizing the importance of using primary resources. She lists more than 100 kinds of records, such as anniversary announcements, bank statements, health records, newspaper clippings, and more.

Kemp, Thomas J. *International Vital Records Handbook.* **Baltimore: Genealogical Publishing Co., 1994.**

Kemp details the procedures for obtaining a birth, marriage, or death certificate in each county, state, province, territory, or country. Application forms are provided, so all you need to do is fill them out and send them to the address listed in the book, along with the appropriate fee.

Kirkham, E. Kay. *The Counties of the United States and Their Genealogical Value.* **Salt Lake City: Deseret Book Co., 1965.**

This book gives a listing of parent county, county seat, and census information for each county.

Lichtman, Allan J. *Your Family History.* **New York: Vintage Books, 1978.**

Lichtman discusses how to use oral history, personal family archives, and public documents to discover your heritage.

Meitzler, Leland K. *On Cemeteries and Funeral Homes* **[videorecording]. Orting, WA: Heritage Quest, 1989.**

An introduction to genealogical research using cemetery and funeral home records. Includes an illustration of tombstone rubbing techniques.

Myrick, Shelby. *Glossary of Legal Terminology.* **Nashville, TN: American Association for State and Local History, 1970.**

Sometimes when you need to look at public records, the terminology can be daunting. This book can help you overcome the difficulties of legalese.

National Archives and Records Administration. *Beginning Your Genealogical Research in the National Archives in Washington.* **Washington, DC: National Archives and Record Administration, 1987.**

This booklet will help you get started searching the National Archives and Records for genealogical information.

Neagles, James C., and Neagles, Lila L. *Locating Your Immigrant Ancestor: A Guide to Naturalization Records.* **Logan, UT: Everton Publishers, 1986.**

Features an index of immigration records dating back to 1837 and listed by state and country. Also explains the immigration process and the immigrant patterns of U.S. history.

Parker, Kenneth B. *Find Your Roots: A Beginner's Kit for Tracing Your Family Tree.* **Southfield, MI: Lezell-Brasch Associates, 1977.**

Great tool for young or beginning genealogists. Includes sample ancestry charts and family group sheets for you to photocopy or use as a model when creating your own.

Petty, Elizabeth. *Genealogist's Address Book.* **Baltimore: Genealogical Publishing Co., 1995.**

This indispensable resource will put a wide variety of genealogical organizations and institutions at your fingertips. Among the sites listed are archives, government agencies, vital records offices, libraries, genealogical societies, historical societies, specific ethnic and religious organizations, computer interest groups, adoption registries, and periodicals and newsletters.

Rabb, Theodore K., and Rotberg, Robert I., eds. *The Family in History.* **New York: Harper & Row, 1973.**

This volume includes the master database of *Genealogy Today, Genealogy Tomorrow,* and the *Computerized Surname Magazines.*

Reed, Evan Laforrest. *Ways and Means of Identifying Ancestors.* **Chicago: Ancestral Publishing & Supply Co., 1947.**

Includes genealogical information in counties in all states east of the Mississippi and in New England towns.

Schreiner-Yantis, Netti. *Genealogical and Local History Books in Print*, **3 vols., 4th ed. Springfield, VA: Schreiner-Yantis, 1990.**

These volumes contain information on genealogical publications, supplies, and services.

Stryker-Rhoda, Harriet. *How to Climb Your Family Tree: Genealogy for Beginners.* **Baltimore: Genealogical Publishing Co., 1992.**

An introduction to the methods and principles of genealogical research. Discusses sources such as census records, church records, vital records, land records, and many kinds of public records.

Westin, Jeane Eddy. *Finding Your Roots: How Every American Can Trace His Ancestors—At Home and Abroad.* **New York: Ballantine Books, 1977.**

Covers everything from how to use the most fundamental records to writing and publishing family history. Contains a list of archives and stores that specialize in genealogical research. Includes information on Chinese immigrants and Chinese Americans.

Where to Write for Vital Records: Births, Deaths, Marriages and Divorces. **Superintendent of Documents, U.S. Government Printing Office, Washington, DC 20402.**

Provides valuable assistance in obtaining and utilizing vital records, both from the government and from source books.

Wright, Norman Edgar. *Adventures in Genealogy: Case Studies in the Unusual.* **Baltimore: Clearfield Company, 1994.**

Wright, an experienced writer and genealogist, takes the reader along on three of his most memorable genealogical hunts. Photographs and facsimiles of documents illustrate the text. The book reads like a detective story, but is also a valuable and enjoyable guide to the research process. Take the opportunity to observe a genealogical master at work.

————. *Preserving Your American Heritage*. **Provo, UT: Brigham Young University Press, 1981.**

An inspiring book to read as you embark upon your research and attempt to answer the question, "why should I trace my roots?" Includes useful information on genealogy procedure and sources.

NATIONAL ARCHIVES

National Archives and Records Administration
Washington, DC 20408

Write for a free catalog of publications and microfilms. The National Archives stores censuses, vital records, ship passenger lists, and other documents required by genealogists. Some examples of their publications are: *Using Records in the National Archives; Getting Started Beginning Your Genealogical Research in the National Archives;* and *Military Service Records in the National Archives.*

NATIONAL ARCHIVES REGIONAL BRANCHES

Central Plains
**2312 East Bannister Road
Kansas City, MO 64131
816-926-6272**

Contains information on Iowa, Kansas, Missouri, Nebraska.

Great Lakes
**7358 South Pulaski Road
Chicago, IL 60629
312-581-7816**

Contains information on Illinois, Indiana, Michigan, Minnesota, Ohio, Wisconsin.

Mid-Atlantic
Ninth and Market Streets

Philadelphia, PA 19107
215-597-3000

Contains information on Delaware, Maryland, Pennsylvania, Virginia, West Virginia.

New England
380 Trapelo Road
Waltham, MA 02154
617-647-8100

Contains information on Connecticut, Maine, Massachusetts, New Hampshire, Rhode Island, Vermont.

Northeast
Building 22—MOT Bayonne
Bayonne, NJ 07002-5388
201-823-7252

Contains information on New Jersey, New York, Puerto Rico, Virgin Islands.

Pacific Northwest
6125 Sand Point Way NE
Seattle, WA 98115
206-526-6507

Contains information on Alaska, Idaho, Oregon, Washington state.

Pacific Sierra
1000 Commodore Drive
San Bruno, CA 94066
415-876-9009

Contains information on Hawaii, Nevada, northern California.

Pacific Southwest
24000 Avila Road
Mailing address: P.O. Box 6719
Laguna Niguel, CA 92677-6719
714-643-4241

Contains information on Arizona, southern California, Nevada's Clark County.

Rocky Mountain
Building 48, Denver Federal Center
Denver, CO 80225
303-236-0818

Contains information on Colorado, Montana, North Dakota, South Dakota, Utah, Wyoming.

Southwest
501 West Felix Street
Mailing address: P.O. Box 6216
Fort Worth, TX 76115
817-334-5525

Contains information on Arkansas, Louisiana, New Mexico, Oklahoma, Texas.

PASSENGER RECORDS

Filby, P. William, ed. *Passenger & Immigration Lists Index: A Reference Guide to Published Lists of About 500,000 Passengers Who Arrived in America in the 17th, 18th, and 19th Centuries*. 3 vols. Detroit: Gale Research Co., 1981.

A comprehensive guide to passenger lists of immigrant ships from the seventeenth through nineteenth centuries.

———, and Meyer, Mary K. *Supplement to Passenger & Immigration List*. Detroit: Gale Research Co., 1987.

An update and supplement to the above volumes.

Tepper, Michael. *American Passenger Arrival Records: A Guide to the Records of Immigrants Arriving at American Ports by Sail and Steam*. Baltimore: Genealogical Publishing Co., 1993.

Gives examples of passenger lists and instruction on how to use them. Covers records from the colonial period to the twentieth century.

CENSUS RECORDS

Lainhart, Ann S. *State Census Records.* **Baltimore: Genealogical Publishing Co., 1992.**

Obtaining census records is essential to your genealogical project. This is the first published comprehensive list of state census records, with information on what sort of data can be found in them.

Thorndale, William, and Dollarhide, William. *Map Guide to the U.S. Federal Censuses: 1790–1920.* **Baltimore: Genealogical Publishing Co., 1991.**

Displays the U.S. county boundaries from 1790 to 1920. Also includes keys to finding census records within a particular area and an index listing all present-day counties.

ADOPTION

Adamec, Christine, and Pierce, William L. *The Encyclopedia of Adoption.* **New York: Facts on File, 1991.**

After giving a brief history of adoption, this book includes explanation of key terms of adoption, names and addresses of organizations like the American Adoption Congress, and a number of records and services. Also provides helpful appendixes and biographies.

Clewer, Lisa Ray. *Official ALMA Searchers' Guide for Adults.* **Los Angeles, CA: Adoptees' Liberty Movement Association, 1982.**

This book is a guide for adoptees who wish to identify their birth parents. If you are a Chinese American adoptee, you will have many opportunities to learn about the culture of your adoptive parents and your birth parents.

Gediman, Judith S., and Brown, Linda P. *BirthBond: Reunions Between Birthparents and Adoptees—What*

Happens After . . . Far Hills, NJ: New Horizon Press, 1989.

> Presents several informative and touching stories of re-unions between adoptees and their birth parents. Includes chapters on what happens after a reunion and why re-unions happen, as well as notes, bibliography, and specific sources.

Lifton, Betty Jean. *Journey of the Adopted Self: A Quest for Wholeness*. New York: Basic Books, 1994.

> This book is broken into three parts that mirror the phases of the adoptee's psychological development: "The Self in Crisis," "The Self in Search," and "The Self in Transfor-mation." The author is an adoptee herself.

Maxtone-Graham, Katrina. *An Adopted Woman*. New York: Coward, McCann & Geoghegan, 1976.

> The author's story of her search for her birth parents, from visiting the agency from which she was adopted to her eventual reunion with her mother.

Powledge, Fred. *So You're Adopted*. New York: Charles Scribner's Sons, 1982.

> Powledge describes the ways in which adoption has changed, provides statistics about adoption, and tells how to search efficiently for roots. Contains a biblio-graphy.

Sachdev, Paul. *Unlocking the Adoption Files*. Lexington, MA: Lexington Books, 1989.

> The first chapter is extremely helpful for beginning re-searchers. Some of the later chapters are a bit technical and intended for scholars and veteran researchers.

Triseliotis, John. *In Search of Origins: The Experi-ences of Adopted People*. Boston: Routledge & Kegan Paul, 1973.

Includes chapters on the differing views of family relationships, self-perception and personal identity, hopes and expectations, the search and aftermath. Contains a bibliography.

ADOPTEE SUPPORT ORGANIZATIONS AND REUNION REGISTRIES

Adoptees and Birthparents in Search
P.O. Box 5551
West Columbia, SC 29171

Adoptees' Birthrights Committee
Box 7213
Metairie, LA 70010

Adoptees' Liberty Movement Association
Box 154, Washington Bridge Station
New York, NY 10033

Adopted and Searching/Adoptee-Birthparent Reunion Registry
401 East 74th St.
New York, NY 10021

Adoption Assistance Agency
18645 Sunburst Street
Northridge, CA 91324

The International Soundex Reunion Registry
P.O. Box 2312
Carson City, NV 89702

INTERNET WEB SITES

Everton Publishers Genealogy Page
http://www.everton.com

This page contains information on getting started as well as specific information on ethnic, religious, and social groups. Includes an online edition of the genealogical magazine *Everton's Genealogical Helper* and provides links to archives, libraries, and other Internet resources.

Genealogy Home Page
ftp://ftp.cac.psu.edu/pub/genealogy
http://ftp.cac.psu.edu/~saw/genealogy.html

By filling out the survey linked to this home page, you will be granted access to many genealogical links, allowing you to communicate with other genealogists, search new databases, and order genealogical software online.

LDS Research Guides
ftp://hipp.etsu.edu/pub/genealogy

This site focuses on the Research Outline Guides produced by the Family History Library in Salt Lake City. Subjects include getting started, frequently asked genealogy questions, and techniques for photograph dating.

National Archives and Records Administration
gopher://gopher.nara.gov
http://www.nara.gov

NARA is the government agency responsible for managing the records of the federal government. Through this page you can find the location and business hours for regional archives or access information on finding and using particular government documents.

U.S. Census Bureau
ftp://gateway.census.gov
http://www.census.gov

From this site you can access statistics about population, housing, economy, and geography as compiled by the U.S. Department of Commerce Bureau of the Census. You can also do specific word searches according to subject or geographic location.

World Wide Web Genealogy Demo Page
http://demo.genweb.org/gene/genedemo.html

This page is still under construction, but its goal is to "create a coordinated, interlinked, distributed worldwide genealogy database." Even in its incomplete form, Gen Web allows you to access all known genealogical databases searchable through the www.

INTERNET SITES OF SPECIAL INTEREST

Asian Net Homepage
http://www.asiannet.com

Claims to be "the largest source of Asian information on the World Wide Web." You can look for information both by country and by subject. Also has a word search option, so you can find data by typing in a keyword.

Chinese Genealogy Surnames
http://nyx10.cs.du.edu:8001/~anon2fda/genealogy.tvt.

Traces the many surnames descended from the Chou Dynasty. Also has information on Chinese genealogy going back to the year 2205 BC in volumes from the Hawaii Chinese Genealogical Society. Includes addresses to write for more information.

Chinese Historical and Cultural Project
http://www.dnai.com~rutledge/CHCP_home.html

The Chinese Historical and Cultural Center (CHCP) is a non-profit organization based in Santa Clara County, California. It works to promote and preserve Chinese and Chinese American history and culture through community outreach activities.

Duen Hsi Yen Home Page
http://www.aloha.com/~yen/Yen_Duen_Hsi.home.html

Duen Hsi Yen has compiled data on many aspects of his family history, including his ancestors' religion and professions. Contains a number of links to the different subject categories.

Hakka Chinese Home Page
http://www.ganet.net/~ITTI/Hakka/general.html.

The home page for the Chang Clan of Ching He Tang. Traces ancestors back 149 generations to Huang Ti, Yellow Emperor. You can send for a twenty-page photostat of a document that traces back to the Sung Dynasty.

Tucson's Chinese Heritage: Tucson's Chinatowns
http://dizzy.library.arizona.edu/images/chiamer/
chinat.html

Photographs and text tell the story of Tucson's earliest Chinese immigrants, describing Chinese American neighborhoods, occupations, and some of the major institutions that fostered a Chinese American community.

Chapter 5
Chinese Clan Registers

Using Chinese sources will be nearly impossible if you are not proficient in the Chinese language. If you do not speak Chinese, find an adult who is willing to help you. Older Chinese are often especially eager to assist a younger person with an interest in his or her Chinese heritage. This can be a valuable opportunity to bridge the generation gap.

Chinese sources are not usually available in public libraries. The demand for such specialized material is not great enough to warrant acquisition and maintenance costs.

Even libraries at major universities do not necessarily have resources for Chinese genealogical research. Only a handful of universities support Chinese materials in great number. Contact your nearest university to see if there is either an East Asian or Chinese Studies program. Some materials may also be available at your local library through interlibrary loan. Check with your librarian.

The Lunar Calendar

Be aware of the differences between the lunar and solar calendars. Until the twentieth century, Chinese used the lunar calendar. Many birthdates, marriage dates, and funerary inscriptions will correspond to lunar dates. Lunar-to-solar conversion tables are available. Before you try to piece together a chronology, determine how your source materials are dated.

The Chinese also compute a person's age differently than in the West. The gestation period is included in the Chinese calculation. A child is born already one year old. At the next New Year's Day according to the lunar calendar, the child enters his or her second year. Therefore, if you were born one day before the New Year, you would be two years old the next day.

History of the *Zupu*

Clan or household registers (known as *zupu* or *jiapu*) have always been valuable resources for historians of China. *Zupu* contain information about clan members and often include a family tree, information about ancestral shrines and gravesites, occupations, and even noteworthy anecdotes about family members.

Prior to the Sung Dynasty (960–1279 AD), *zupu* were primarily used to designate generational relationships between family members and to record marriages. By the Ming (1368–1644 AD) and Ch'ing (1644–1912 AD) dynasties, the *zupu's* function had diversified. Many registers were altered to glorify a clan's reputation. Illegitimate births were probably not noted. Women were also generally overlooked unless they were particularly accomplished by the standards of Confucian virtue. From the Wei to the T'ang Dynasty (220–618 AD), women were mentioned only in the context of marriage. In spite of its patriarchal bias, the clan register, or *zupu*, is invaluable.

There were several reasons for maintaining clan registers. Being listed in a *zupu* was a sign of social recognition. The *zupu* glorified a man's educational status. It recorded ancestral traditions to be handed to posterity. Even today, the *zupu* contains crucial information about a family's particular customs and practices. The Wu family of Ilan, Taiwan, for example, recorded in their *zupu* the reason they celebrated Buddhist Day one day earlier than usual: they kept their family business open on the holiday.

Exclusion from the *zupu* was also used to punish criminals. Individuals were grouped according to generational hierarchy, and the ostracized were unable to have their names listed. The Chen family of Anping declared in their *zupu*: "If anyone was deviant, he was not registered. In this way, criminals and heinous crimes were punished. If one traverses elders, is punished by the law, or is unfilial, he shall

Traditional *zupus* tend to focus on the men of a family. This undated photo shows a Chinese father and his children.

not be considered part of the brotherhood. He will not be entered in the register." This kind of statement in a *zupu* was meant for future generations to read (and heed).

Using the *Zupu*

If you would like to locate your *zupu*, the first thing you need to do is find out where in China your family originated. Ask your parents or grandparents to be as precise as possible; *zupus* are geographically specific.

Some *zupus* may exist in translation. However, most Chinese genealogical sources remain untranslated. Many *zupus* are handed down from generation to generation. Ask an older relative if your family has one.

Living family members were responsible for updating the information in a *zupu*. Usually one member of the family is elected to compile and update it. Sometimes, Chinese historians are appointed to compile *zupus*. You may discover that your family still maintains a *zupu*. The following section is designed to introduce you to the general format of a *zupu*, using a real example. Although format may vary from region to region in China, all *zupus* contain similar information.

Zupus in print today have usually been edited or recompiled from several other *zupus* and clan histories. For purposes of illustration, let us say that your last name is Chen and you are looking in an East Asian collection for your *zupu*. The *zupu* we have selected for illustrative purposes was pulled from the stacks of the East Asian Library at the University of California–Berkeley.

Chen is a very common surname among Chinese. We used the library computer and searched according to the Library of Congress subject field: "Genealogy—China." The entries that came up on the screen were romanized Chinese titles. The Chen Clan Register we selected was romanized as Chen Chia P'u. This exact same source could have appeared in English as Chen Jia Pu. First of all, you would need to remember that *jiapu* is an alternative way of referring to *zupu*. You would also need to become functional using the various methods of Chinese romanization. You will probably need to ask the librarian who specializes in the Chinese collection to help you find what you are looking for.

Let's assume that, with the help of the librarian, you have the *zupu* in hand. On the very first page of the prologue, the compiler indicates that this *zupu* is for the Chens of I-men Jiangzhou. If you do not know exactly where your family originated, it may be difficult to search for your family's *zupu*. Usually, *zupu* titles use the surname followed by the family's place of origin.

The prologue of a *zupu* usually contains historical information about the lineage, such as who the founding ancestor is believed to be. The opening lines of the Chen *zupu* read: "As a country must have a history, and as a family must have historical records, so must we record past dealings to enlighten future generations, allowing them to know their origins and deepen their ties with the past. Our founding ancestor was Man Gong, or Yu Diwu. He was born as Wei

Na of the Wei Clan. After Zhou Su Wang (another name for Man Gong) conquered Yen Zhou he was bequeathed a fiefdom at Chen, and was worshiped as Diwu. After nine years, Man Gong died and was conferred the posthumous title Hu, thus making him Hu Man Gong. At the end of the Spring-Autumn era, the region was unified by Chu. Throughout the Warring States and Ch'in eras, descendants of Man Gong were referred to as the Chen clan."

The *zupu* in the example above was recompiled in 1983. Stories about a founding ancestor may be fictitious. According to the *zupu*, Man Gong lived before the Spring-Autumn era, which dates back to 722 BC. Often, for political reasons, a family might select an ancestor as a symbol of prestige. The text implies that Man Gong held a fiefdom, which would have qualified him as a prestigious individual.

Zupu **Table of Contents**

Extensive *zupus* compiled in the twentieth century usually contain a helpful table of contents. The first few sections of the Chen family *zupu* deal with family history and founding ancestors. Prominent descendants of Man Gong are named and described. The founding ancestors are listed according to generation. A sweeping history of the family serves as introductory material. Classical Chinese rather than modern Chinese is used to describe how the founding patriarchs made the Chen family great. The old style of writing gives the text the feel of historical annals. These historical sections are referred to as *shi shi*.

The *zupu* is difficult even for Chinese natives to read. It would be like asking an English speaker to read and comprehend the language of Chaucer. Most readers today would have to rely heavily on footnotes to help them through the material. Modern compilations of ancient Chinese documents usually are footnoted or translated into modern Chinese. The Chen *zupu* happens to be an ambitious compilation of many sources that pertain to the Chen family. Not all *zupus* are as extensive.

Sometimes living family members contribute to the *zupu*.

If your *zupu* has been compiled from several sources, there will be repetitious information that, with some experience, can be skimmed. Following the introductory segment of the Chen *zupu*, the next main section contains historiographical records. A historiography is, essentially, a history of history. The Chen's historiography tells about how information in the *zupu* was collected.

The Family Tree: A Patrilineal History

Unless they were paragons of Confucian virtue, women were omitted from the *zupu*. The Chen *zupu* does not deviate from this convention. It provides us with a detailed family tree that includes the surnames of related feudal princes. The family tree covers ninety-two generations. Of course, only prominent male family members are listed. Most of them held official ranks. Dukes and sons of dukes are listed in the Chen *zupu*.

It is interesting to note the practice of generational naming. Until the twentieth century, children born in the same generation within a family shared the same Chinese character in their names. Most Chinese names contain three characters, the surname character followed by two characters in the given name. It is usually the second character that is shared. For example, in the Chen *zupu* the eighty-seventh generation is the "Wan" generation. Thus, some of the names are Chen Wan-wan, Chen Wan-zhuang, and so forth.

Following the extensive ninety-two-generation chart, the next section provides more detailed information for every single person listed. Perhaps you are interested in finding out more about a person of the ninetieth generation. You would look through the material until you found the heading for the ninetieth generation (*jiu shi shi*). Each individual is considered a subheading within the generation. Here is a translated sample of what you would find: (Name) De Gui Gong: alternate designations, Mao Zhai. The son of Zhu Wen Gong. Born in the Yuan Dynasty, during the ninth year of the reign of the Da De Emperor (1304 AD). Died in the sixth year of the Hung Wu Emperor and was buried in the township of Shi Ma in the Heng Jing Mountains. Married Lady Huang, born in eleventh year of the reign of Da De. Their son was Da Bi.

Ancient geographical place names are not always traceable today. However, in some cases the modern compilers have included a map of likely locations of ancient townships superimposed on a modern map.

Sometimes, replicas of ancient *zupus* contain elaborate diagrams of the clan compounds that map out where each branch of the clan resided in relation to other family members. Chinese clans usually lived in walled compounds or villages.

Historical Annals: *Shi Shi*

In ancient China, a court historian had the job of recording the accomplishments of the preceding dynasty. The most famous Chinese historian of ancient times was Sima Qian (c. 193–145 BC). He lived during the Han Dynasty (206 BC–220 AD). Sima's literary style became a standard for future histories. Sima would intermix historical events with moralistic commentary. Many *zupus* contain historical accounts that reflect Sima's legacy.

The Chen family *zupu* contains a history, or *shi shi*, with many miniature biographical sketches of prominent ancestors. It sounds something like this: Chen Wan Gong was the youngest son of Chen Wen Gong. His mother was Madame Cai. When Wen Gong passed on, Wan Gong's eldest brother Chen Bao came to power and called himself Xun Gong. Xun Gong and Wan Gong were born of different mothers. Then, Xun Gong became ill. Somebody in the Cai family killed Xun Gong and Tai Zi Mian succeeded Chen Wan Gong.

The histories contain interesting stories about family intrigue. Following a narrative like the one illustrated above, every history must conclude with a commentary that alludes to legendary historical figures. These figures are held up as models for posterity. The Chen family *zupu* is no different: "The Historian says: The virtue of Yao was sung for three generations. When Tien Chang usurped the throne, and established a country, those who were landholders were not wanting."

The *zupu* is a rich source of information. It reflects the richness of written materials in Chinese culture. Even though you may never find a *zupu* for your family, you can use what you have learned here to structure your own genealogy. You can develop a family tree that will, in other sections, include more information about each ancestor. You can preface your genealogy with a page about yourself. Write stories about your favorite relatives. You may want to collect, for example, humorous anecdotes about your ancestors. Or, maybe you just want to record vital statistics.

Visiting China

Some Chinese American families make regular visits to China to visit relatives. If this is the case with your family, you may have a unique opportunity to conduct interviews with relatives in China and perhaps even to access Chinese records sources.

If your family is not planning a trip to China in the near future, you may decide to plan a visit on your own as part of your genealogical research. If you wish to plan such a visit, Chinese genealogists recommend contacting relatives far in advance to let them know of your plans.

Your visit may include a stop in your ancestral village, where you may be able to view valuable bits of family history such as family plots in the local cemetery, a clan temple, an ancestral hall, or ancestral tablets. An ancestral tablet can list several generations of a male lineage. Walking in the land of your ancestors amid relics of the past will be an exciting and rewarding experience.

You may encounter stumbling blocks in your research. For example, Chinese officials may be reluctant to allow you access to certain records. Other records may not be available to you at all.

Libraries and genealogical collections may have many ancient and important genealogical materials. Unfortunately, many of these materials were burned during the 1950s when there was an attempt by the Communist Party to eliminate publications believed to represent a feudal mentality. In 1949, some family histories were moved from Mainland China to Taiwan. Many other clan and family genealogies continue to be published in Taiwan. If any branches of your family live or have lived in Taiwan, you may find genealogical materials on your family there. If you visit Taiwan, plan a visit to the National Central Library in Taipei.

Resources

CHINESE GENEALOGY

Beard, Timothy Field, and Demong, Denise. *How to Find Your Family Roots*. **New York: McGraw-Hill, 1977.**

> The chapter "Tracing Your Family Roots Abroad" includes lists of resources about China, Taiwan, and Tibet, and provides specific advice for Chinese Americans.

Chang Liao. *Shih tsupu*. **Taichung: Hsinyuan tung chu pan she, 1965.**

> This is the *zupu* of the Chang family of Taichung, Taiwan, as compiled by the Changs themselves. The character "Chang" is a common surname composed of the two components, "arrow" and "long." The compilers were Chang Liao Chien and Chang Fu Tang. (In Chinese.)

Chang Pi-te. *Taiwan kung tsang tsu pu chieh-ti*. **Taipei, 1969.**

> Includes 130 annotated Chinese genealogies for Taiwanese families. By knowing your family's surname or the region they came from, you may be able to find useful information. This collection includes some of the most common surnames of Taiwan, such as Li and Chen. These genealogies follow a format like that discussed in the sections about *zupu*. (In Chinese.)

Chao Chen-chi. *Catalogue of Chinese Genealogies in Taiwan*. **Taipei, 1986.**

> A more recently published reference for those considering serious Chinese genealogical work, this book is a guide to where actual genealogies are kept. It is possible that you

will be able to find copies of some of these genealogies in the U.S. Library of Congress. Many Chinese genealogies are also kept at the National Library of Taiwan, in Taipei. If you have friends or relatives going to Taiwan for a visit, they might be able to access your family's genealogy.

Ching, Frank. *Ancestors: 900 Years in the Life of a Chinese Family.* **New York: Ballantine, 1989.**

A Chinese American author traces his genealogical tree over nine centuries.

Goodsell, Willystine, trans. *History of the Family as a Social and Educational Institution.* **Shanghai: Shanghai wen i chu pan she, 1989.**

Very few Chinese academic works have been translated into English. This book can provide you with insight on how Chinese research scholars view the evolution of the Chinese family. (Translation from the Chinese.)

I-lan Chang shih tsu pu. **(Special collection of University of California, UCLA call number CS 1169.5 C43 1983).**

Zupu of the Changs of Ilan, Taiwan. This is a real twentieth-century *zupu*, held exclusively at the UCLA collection. If you know that your family came from Ilan, there would be a good case for you to have access to this document. (In Chinese.)

Jao, Tsung-i. *Tang Sung mu chih.* **Hong Kong: Chinese University Press, 1981.**

This book contains grave inscriptions of the T'ang and Sung dynasties. Grave inscriptions can be used not so much for personal genealogies, but more for an understanding of how the individual was eulogized by Chinese society. (In Chinese.)

Kung, Te-cheng. *Kung-tzu shih chia pu.* **Chi-nan shih: Shantung yu I shu she, 1990.**

This is the *zupu* of descendants of Confucius. The Kung

family have always been proud of their relation to Confucius. Whether or not blood relation can be proved, this document demonstrates the importance of lineage to the Chinese. Founding ancestors usually become symbolic leaders of clans with the same surname. (In Chinese.)

Lin, Tien-yu. *Kuang-tung Chung-shan hsien ni-wan hsiang Lin shih chia pu.* **(Special collection at UCLA library).**

This is the *zupu* for the Lins of Chung-shan county, Guangdong province. If you are a Lin (the Chinese character is written by putting two "wood" radicals together) from Guangdong, or Canton, there would be good reason for you to look at this rare document. (In Chinese.)

Lo, Hsiang-lin. *Chung-kuo tsu-pu yen chiu.* **Hong Kong: Chung-kuo Shueh-she, 1971.**

Provides a list of genealogical materials in the Guangdong Provincial Library. Also includes some materials about the Hakka, a Chinese minority group. (In Chinese.)

———. "The Extent and Preservation of Genealogical Records in China." Salt Lake City: World Conference on Records, 1969.

This is a booklet that can be ordered from the LDS Family History Library, or found in one of its branch libraries. It is considered the definitive work on Chinese genealogy.

———. "The History and Arrangement of Chinese Genealogies" and "The Preservation of Genealogical Records in China." In *Studies in Asian Genealogy*, ed. Spencer J. Palmer. Provo, UT: Brigham Young University Press, 1972.

These articles have been recommended by a number of genealogical societies as good research guides for Chinese genealogies. Because the nature of Chinese genealogies is complex, it is a good idea to obtain as much general information as possible before delving deeply into research.

Low, Jeanie W. Chooey. *China Connection: Finding Ancestry Roots for Chinese America.* **San Francisco: JWC Low Co., 1994.**

This source offers important tips for embarking on a Chinese genealogical search.

Meskill, Johanna. "The Chinese Genealogy as a Research Source." In *Family and Kinship in Chinese Society***, ed. Maurice Freedman. Stanford: Stanford University Press, 1970.**

Professor Meskill gives some pointers on how to get the most out of using *zupu* for research.

Nelson, H. G. H. "Ancestor Worship and Burial Practices." In *Religion and Ritual in Chinese Society***, ed. Arthur P. Worl. Stanford: Stanford University Press, 1974.**

A fascinating article about how the Chinese manipulate genealogies for social purposes. Genealogies were used to glorify illustrious ancestors.

Reed, Robert D. *How and Where to Research Your Ethnic-American Cultural Heritage—Chinese Americans.* **Saratoga, CA: R. Reed, 1979.**

A short history of Chinese Americans, plus genealogical sources and a bibliography.

Telford, Ted. *Chinese Genealogies at the Genealogical Society of Utah.* **Taipei: Cheng-wen Publishing Co., 1983.**

A comprehensive reference source. Includes a place names index arranged by province. Place name indexes are particularly helpful if you are tracing maternal relatives whose surnames you may not know.

HELPFUL ORGANIZATIONS

The following organizations may be able to help answer your research questions.

Aloha Chapter Memorial Library
(Daughters of the American Revolution)
1914 Makiki Heights Drive
Honolulu, HI 96822

An excellent source of records for Hawaiians of Chinese ancestry.

Center for Chinese Research Materials
P.O. Box 3090
Oakton, VA 22124

Contact this center to see whether any of their holdings might have relevance to your research project.

Chinese American Librarian Association
2000 Jed Smith Drive
Sacramento, CA 95819

Chinese American librarians are especially qualified to help you find the materials you need. Write to this organization for referrals and for answers to specific research questions.

Chinese Culture Association
P.O. Box 1272
Palo Alto, CA 94392-1272

This organization promotes Chinese culture.

Chinese Culture Foundation of San Francisco
750 Kearny Street
San Francisco, CA 94108

Write for information about the foundation's genealogy research programs for youths.

Chinese Historical Society of America
650 Commercial Street
San Francisco, CA 94111

Address your questions on Chinese history to the experts here.

Chinese Information and Culture Center
1230 Avenue of the Americas
New York, NY 10020-1513

This center may be especially helpful if you are planning a visit to China. They can provide information on travel and events in China.

**Chinese Language Teachers Association
1200 Academy Street
Kalamazoo, MI 49006**

If you are interested in learning Chinese, contact this association for a referral to a Chinese-language teacher.

**Chou Clansmen Association of America
P.O. Box 4604
Honolulu, HI 96812-4604**

Even if you are not of the Chou clan, this association may be able to advise you on researching your own clan ties, particularly if your ancestors lived in Hawaii.

**Columbia University
East Asian Library
116th Street and Broadway
New York, NY 10027**

This library has Chinese genealogies in its collection.

**Family History Library
Church of Jesus Christ of Latter-day Saints
50 North West Temple Street
Salt Lake City, UT 84150**

The FHL has local family history centers in the United States and other countries. They maintain large holdings of catalogs and microfilmed records on immigrants, including Chinese Americans. You can order their research papers on genealogical research: *The Content and Use of Chinese Local History*, by Tsun Leng, *Arrangement of Chinese Clan Genealogies*, by Hsiang-lin Lo, and *Genealogical Sources of Chinese Immigrants* by Thomas W. Chinn.

**Harvard University
Yenching Institute
Cambridge, MA 02138**

This institute's holdings include complete Chinese genealogies.

Hawaii Chinese History Center
111 North King Street
Honolulu, HI 96817

This history center offers booklets on Chinese genealogy, such as *Chinese Genealogy and Family Book Guide* by Jean Bergen Ohai.

Organization of Chinese Americans
10001 Connecticut Avenue NW, #707
Washington, DC 20036

This organization offers programs for senior citizens, new immigrants, women, and students. They have a scholarship for Chinese American high school students.

Research and Statistics Office
P.O. Box 3378
Honolulu, Hawaii 96801

Contact this office when tracing your Chinese roots in Hawaii. They can help you locate birth, marriage, and death certificates.

Chapter 6
Local Gazetteers

The local Chinese gazetteer, or *di fang zhi*, is another source
of use to the genealogist. A gazetteer is a geographical dictionary. Professional historians have devoted their lives to
the study of these sources. They are about as difficult to
access and use as are *zupu*, but *di fang zhi* are important
because they give us information about specific localities.
There is a good selection of *di fang zhi* available in the
United States.

Di fang zhi began as documents that mapped out and
defined the perimeters of specific geographical areas.
Chinese officials compiled information about an area, much
as our government collects survey information. Over the
years, *di fang zhi* diversified and came to include information
about an area's climate, topography, and local produce. By
the Sung Dynasty (960–1279 AD), *di fang zhi* contained
maps, information about the economy, local handicrafts,
culture, architecture, government officials, folklore, and
noteworthy technological advancements. As far as we know,
during the Sung Dynasty about 700 local gazetteers were
compiled. Local gazetteers were compiled into the twentieth
century.

If you are having a difficult time picturing the regions
where your Chinese ancestors lived, the *di fang zhi* might
provide valuable information. Because the gazetteer was not
considered an official history, its compilers had little reason
to present deliberately biased views or false information. In
addition to a basic description of a region, the *di fang zhi*
contains information concerning the census, farm and excise
taxes, military affairs, and history.

Local Gazetteers in U.S. Libraries

The Library of Congress was the first U.S. library to collect Chinese materials, starting in 1869. Diplomats and academics often returned from China with Chinese materials, among which were *di fang zhi*. Many ancient Chinese documents were destroyed during the Cultural Revolution in China in the 1960s. Revolting against traditional culture, the Communist Chinese government destroyed anything associated with the imperial regime. Fortunately, American and British bibliophiles avidly collected Chinese materials during the late nineteenth and early twentieth centuries.

Most *di fang zhi* are housed in either national or university research facilities. Below is a bibliographic table containing a list of some *di fang zhi* available in U.S. libraries.

Title and Date of Compilation	Province	U.S. Library Location
Bai Cheng Yen Shui 1690	Jiangsu	Library of Congress (LC)
Cai Feng Lei Ji 1755	Jiangsu	LC
Qing Feng Jing Zhi 1873	Jiangsu	LC
Jiang Yin Xian Zhi 1656	Jiangsu	Harvard University (H)
Zhe Jiang Si Bian 1934	Zhejiang	LC
Zhe Jiang Tong Zhi	Zhejiang	H
Yue Zhong Za Shi 1694	Zhejiang	LC
Hu Shu Xiao Zhi 1896	Zhejiang	Columbia University (C)
Tong Xi Ji Lue 1797	Zhejiang	C
Sui Chuan Xian Zhi	Jiangxi	C
Han Yang Xian Zhi	Hubei	University of Chicago
Hui Tong Xiang Zhi 1820	Hunan	H

Hunan Dili Zhi 1833	Hunan	H
Chengdu Fu Zhi 1621	Sichuan	LC
Fujian Tong Zhi	Fujian	H
Taiwan San Bian 1927	Taiwan	LC
Long Chuan Xian Zhi 1739	Guangdong	LC
Chao Cheng Bei Cai Lu 1861	Guangdong	C
Tian Ze 1923	Yunnan	LC
Qing Yuan Xian Shi Qing Diao Cha 1939	Hebei	LC
Hebei Shen Dingxing Xian Shi Qing Tiao Cha 1939	Hebei	LC
Shou Kuang Xian Zhi 1755	Shandong	LC
Qingdao Dao 1936	Shandong	LC
Jiao Zhou Zhi 1824	Shandong	LC
Mi Xian Zhi 1750	Honan	LC
Gu Shi Xian Zhi 1778	Honan	LC
Wu An Feng Tu Ji 1906	Honan	LC
Shanxi Si Bian 1939	Shanxi	LC
Duan Zhou Zhi 1764	Shanxi	LC
Long De Xian Du Zhi 1826	Gansu	LC
Xiao He Cheng Zhi 1909	Gansu	LC

Using *Di fang zhi*

You can enlist the help of an older relative when needing to access local gazetteers. Go to the local library and see if a librarian might help you find a listing of the East Asian collections in the United States. If you or your local library can access the Internet, you can hook up to the Library of Congress home page at http://lcweb.loc.gov/homepage/

online.html. Then you will be able to search the Library of Congress catalog, using the name of your ancestors' town or region to determine if the Library holds a *di fang zhi* that might be of use to you. Once you obtain a *di fang zhi* for the region your Chinese ancestors came from, sit down with an elder and flip through the sections. Review the sections that contain information about specific individuals. Browse through other sections that might appeal to you. Sometimes *di fang zhi* contain information about ominous or strange events that have occurred in the history of an area.

Resources

LOCAL GAZETTEERS

Chu, Tung tsu. *Local Gazetteers: An Introductory Syllabus.* **(Special collection at University of California–Berkeley East Asian Library, call number DS 705.c54 1960.)**

> Professor Chu is an expert in Chinese local history. His course syllabus would be the place for any beginner to start. You may want to try calling the East Asian Library at 415-642-2556 to see if they would be willing to lend you the syllabus through interlibrary loan.

————. *Local Government in China Under the Ching.* **Cambridge, MA: Council on East Asian Studies, Harvard University Press, 1988.**

> This is a classic study of local government in China using local gazetteers as sources. Professor Chu has pioneered the effort in the United States to study local Chinese history. Anyone interested in using local gazetteers should read this book. Chu talks about the role of the Yamen, or local government headquarters.

Chang, Fang-hua. *A Checklist of Chinese Local Histories.* **Berkeley and Stanford, CA: Berkeley-Stanford Joint East Asia Center, 1980.**

> Many scholars have attempted to catalog the whereabouts of various local gazetteers. Gazetteers have been literally spread all over the United States and China. Many American scholars brought local histories to the United States, which is why the Library of Congress has an extensive collection. This book can give you an idea of what is available in the local history collections at Berkeley and Stanford.

Chung kuo ti fang chih tsung lan, 1949–1987. Hofei: Huang shan shu she chu pan, 1988.

A listing of twentieth-century gazetteers (in Chinese). Gazetteer compilation continues today. Still representative of regions in China, the modern-day gazetteer includes much more statistical information than gazetteers of the past.

Church of Jesus Christ of Latter-day Saints. *Genealogical Department Preliminary List of Chinese Local Histories at the Genealogical Society of Utah.* Salt Lake City: Church of Jesus Christ of Latter-day Saints, 1987.

The Mormons are avid compilers of genealogical information. An East Asian library at a university might carry this resource. Check also at the LDS Family History Library or at one of their many local Family History Centers.

Library of Congress. *Kuo hui tu shu kuan tsang Chung-kuo fang chih mu lu.* Washington, DC: U.S. Government Printing Office, 1942.

A listing of the local gazetteers in the U.S. Library of Congress. The gazetteers are listed by region. You need to know Chinese (or be assisted by a Chinese speaker) to use this guide.

Chapter 7
Oral History

Oral history is a useful alternative when written sources are either scanty or difficult to use. When written genealogical sources are not readily accessible, probing the memories of parents and grandparents for valuable information may be your only choice. Most of the time, people love to talk about themselves. Sharing the past with you will give your elders a chance to sift through their complex thoughts and emotions. In sharing their experiences with you, your elders will be making history right before your eyes.

Oral history paints a fuller picture of relatives who might otherwise be just names. It may also provide you with names previously unknown to you. One of your relatives might disclose something that will lead you to other information. Family members who are no longer living may be "brought to life" through anecdotes told by other relatives.

Let's say you are interviewing an aunt. She may mention other relatives whom you do not know as well. You can jot down these names and try to set up interviews with them. Just because you do not know them well does not mean that they will not know a lot about your family. If your aunt mentions a deceased individual, you might then turn to written sources to glean more information. Oral history can be used in conjunction with written materials. Every name that comes up in an oral history has potential. If you are interested in creating a pedigree chart, or even in imitating a Chinese *zupu*, your first task should be to ask your subject to list every relative he or she can think of.

Preparing for an Interview

Before you interview somebody, put yourself in the position

Your elders may be able to provide you with valuable insight on times past and on the details of the lives of family members. Above, "Grandmother" Moy reads news of the war between China and Japan to her grandchildren in Philadelphia in 1937.

of a journalist. You should have an idea of what kind of information you would like to obtain. You should also be prepared to deviate from your original outline. Many people will wish to share only a certain part of themselves. You should respect their privacy; do not persist in asking about a subject if you sense that the interviewee is uncomfortable. You need to develop an interview agenda (a list of questions) simply as a point of departure. From there, allow for spontaneity. Make sure you and the interviewee are comfortable. Think about where it would be best to conduct your interview. Be accommodating. Offer to come to the interviewee's home, if this is most convenient for him or her.

Some people like to be approached formally, whereas others may wish to chat with you casually. Be flexible, and adapt your own style to that of your interviewee.

Ask whether you can tape record the interview. Take notes at the same time; this may help to trigger more questions as well as giving you a written record of the interview in case something goes wrong with the tape recording. Although transcribing (writing out) a tape is time-consuming, it will ensure that you capture all that is said.

Interview Questions

Begin by making a list of basic questions about birthplace, family, occupation, or any other essential facts you need to know. This may be all you need if your subject is outgoing and willing to share information. You might also prepare a list of things to ask during lulls in the conversation. If your interviewee gets tongue-tied, ask questions such as, "What were some of the biggest turning points in your life?" "If you could live your life again, what would you change?" Questions such as these will usually cause a spark. Look quickly over the information you have already garnered. Most likely, you will come up with new questions based on earlier answers. Try to ask open-ended questions: that is, questions that can't be answered by a simple yes or no. Ask questions that include the words "how" and "why."

Here are some ideas for starting questions:

1) Tell me about your (or your parents' or grandparents') immigration to this country. What were the main reasons for coming to the United States?

2) What was your first impression of the United States? What were your greatest fears? What surprised you the most?

3) What do you think it means to be Chinese American? How has growing up in a bicultural home affected you? How do you preserve elements of your Chinese heritage?

4) If you could live your life over, what would you change about it?

5) When you were growing up, to whom did you turn to for advice? Which family members were you closest to?

6) How do you want to be remembered?

7) Do you know of any relative who is compiling or has compiled a genealogy? Are there any other genealogical materials available about our family?

8) Name all the places you have lived in your life. What was your favorite place? Why?

9) Name all the relatives you can think of and the places they have lived in the United States. How many generations back can you name? If you cannot remember names, do you remember anything in particular that might help me track these people down, such as occupation or residence?

10) From what region in China did our ancestors come?

11) Have you travelled back to China? Why or why not? If so, what was it like?

Interviewing by Mail

If your relatives do not live near you, it may not be feasible to plan to interview them in person. But that doesn't mean that you cannot approach them for information. If you have access to e-mail, for example, this can be a convenient and quick way to contact distant relatives. Or, try the more old-fashioned approach: Send a letter.

Write a few paragraphs describing your project and the goals you hope to attain. You may choose to keep your request open-ended, asking your relatives to write personal histories of themselves in their own style. But if you want to be sure that you will get specific information, it is probably best to use a more structured format by including a list of direct questions. Be sure to make it as easy as possible for your relatives to reply by leaving spaces for them to fill in and enclosing a stamped, self-addressed envelope. If possible, call them a few weeks after you send the letter to make sure that it has been received and to ascertain your relative's willingness to participate in your project. Do not push them to respond if they seem unwilling or too busy; you don't want to offend anyone by being too aggressive. Understand that they may simply be hesitant to contribute to a project when they're not sure if it is going to get off the ground. For people with this mindset, you might back off for the time being and send them an update in a few months when you

---

Date

                                           Your address

Interviewee's name
Interviewee's address

Dear _____ (Name of interviewee):

I am researching the genealogy of the _____ family. As part of my research, I am collecting information from family members. I am interested in the facts of your life, your memories of your own experiences, and your memories of other family members.

    I hope that you will be so kind as to take the time to fill out the enclosed questionnaire. If you have any other information to add, please feel free to attach it on a separate sheet of paper. I have enclosed a stamped, self-addressed envelope for your convenience.

    Thank you for taking the time to assist me in this valuable project. I will keep you updated on my progress and will of course provide you with a copy of our family history when it is finished. I would very much appreciate receiving your answers to my questions within two months, or at your earliest convenience.

Very truly yours,

_____
(Your name)

have completed more work on your project. They may be more willing to help out when they see that you are truly dedicated to the project and plan to see it through to a conclusion.

Some people work better under a deadline. If they receive your questionnaire with no indication of when you want it back, they may simply set it aside until they have some "free time." But for most people, free time is hard to come by, and something that has been put aside may be forgotten by the time that free time finally rolls around.

Opposite this page is an example of a letter proposing an "interview by mail." This can easily be adapted for e-mail by attaching your questionnaire to the letter document and asking your interviewee to fill in answers and send the document back to you in an e-mail reply.

Transcribing the Interview

Depending upon how long your interview lasts, you may want to consider recording it on tape. Make absolutely certain, however, that the person knows he or she is being taped and approves of it.

After each interview, examine your written notes thoroughly. Fill in any gaps you might have glossed over during the interview. It is probably not a good idea to let your tapes sit for too long before you transcribe them. Transcribing will put the interview in a useful form and allow you to organize the information collected from the interview.

Your work will be greatly facilitated by a word processor, which will help you store your information and retrieve it quickly later. If you don't have a computer, a typewriter will do just fine. You can even write out interviews by hand. Transcribing every single word may not be necessary. Your motive for creating an oral history may be just to get some names. If this is the case, you may not even want to transcribe your interviews. Just review the tape and jot down necessary information.

Be creative. Maybe your interviews tell a great deal about certain relatives. You can rewrite the information in a story format and append it to a simple family tree. This format would, in a way, be like your own modern rendition of a *zupu*. You might want to divide your family tree by generations, like a *zupu*. With each generation, you can develop a key that corresponds to a story.

Genealogies can be extremely detailed both horizontally and vertically. You can trace back many generations while at the same time learn more about your ancestors as individuals.

Example of an Oral History Project

Your genealogy remains most meaningful to yourself. You have decided to search for your roots. How you gather information is entirely up to you. After you have found some materials, the challenge lies in assembling and presenting your findings. One way to do this is to learn from many years of research that social scientists have conducted in the field of oral history.

I have personally used oral history as a way to add biographical data to a genealogy. In 1987, during my last year of college, I was granted a special scholarship to create an oral history. I wanted to interview my grandfather, who served as a major general in the Nationalist Chinese armed forces under Chiang Kai-shek.

I was to spend an entire summer in Taiwan collecting information. In the dreadful humidity of August in Taipei, I insisted that my mother accompany me to serve as interpreter. It never occurred to me that these interviews would forge a new path for me. It was in that summer that I decided to pursue graduate studies in Chinese history. After a long summer of needing an interpreter, I felt the frustration of not being able to communicate with my grandfather fluently.

I recall how many of my American friends did not have to contend with a language barrier when dealing with grandparents. By contrast, I was not only geographically distant from my stoic Chinese grandfather, but also culturally out of touch. Grandfather would shake his head with disapproval as

I maintained a blank look on my face. He kept telling my mother what a shame it was that his grandchildren did not speak Chinese. It was certainly not out of shame that I chose to pursue Chinese history. Grandfather's colorful life was enough to entice me. My intent to create an oral history was initially rather romantic. I wanted to know more about my roots. You are probably asking similar questions: Who were my forebears? What kind of people were they?

As you create your genealogy, you should allow it to grow spontaneously. When I began my oral history project, I never intended it to be more than a direct transcription of the interview. Over two years, my project evolved from an oral history to a study of the meaning of autobiography in Chinese culture. Oral history can be used as a backbone for more ambitious projects.

Before you begin your oral history, think about some topics you might like to discuss. For instance, talk about an heirloom, or anything that might bring out an interesting angle of your family history. Before you interview people for an oral history, take the time to jot down ten major questions. These questions can be very broad and should be issue-related. Below are excerpts from my proposal.

> My aunt was recently telling me that Grandfather took her to the National Palace Museum in Taipei and showed her a painting. He told her that the man in the painting was our founding ancestor. Pictured was a hermit-sage on a mountain top. A calligraphied couplet read, in translation, "Mountains high, waters eternal," which was presumably a motto eulogizing the lofty nature of this ancestor's virtue and the eternality of his soul. This hermit-sage was supposedly related to a T'ang Dynasty emperor. He forsook worldly pursuits for a life of contemplation. Grandfather genuinely accepts the idea that his origins can be traced back to this intellectual hermit-sage.
>
> In *The Education of Henry Adams*, Adams wrote, "This is the story of an education, and the person or persons who figure in it are supposed to have values only as edu-

cators of the educated." My goal is to determine what part the hermit-sage played as "educator" to my grandfather. I would also like to know how Chiang Kai-shek affected my grandfather's life.

In the Chinese tradition, the disciple/teacher relationship holds great cultural significance. *The Analects* report that Confucius once said: "Shen! My teaching contains one principle that runs through it all." "Yes, indeed Master," replied Tseng Tzu. When Confucius had left the room the disciples asked: "What did he mean?" Tseng Tzu replied, "Our Master's teaching is simply this: loyalty and reciprocity."

At the beginning of the project, I did not know what to expect. All I knew was that I needed answers to an unbelievable number of questions.

Summer in the Study

My grandfather gracefully fanned himself as he sat erect in a wicker chair. He was in his eighties and more than eager to relate his life story. In fact, at his age he was consumed with self-recollection. At the time, Grandfather was finishing his memoirs to be passed on to his family.

To give you an idea of how conversations in your interview can flow, here is a part of my transcription. Your relatives will have equally interesting things to share with you if they are willing. Some people may not want to express themselves verbally, in which case you may want to have them write about themselves. Others may not want to share things with you. Whatever may be the case, you need to respect the feelings of your relatives.

Question: What in your opinion is the underlying ethic in Chinese education?

Yein (Grandfather): As far as ethics are concerned, I really do not have much to say. But politically, in my opinion, education should be for the betterment of the people. I grew up in rural China. When I first went to school, I understood little. Being educated results only from hard study; only then can one be enlightened. I remember the education I received in the year the Ch'ing Dynasty collapsed (1911). I was reading the Four Books, after which I read the *I-jing*. In those days, a teacher would have us read these books and memorize every single word by rote. In our youth, we understood little. These ancient Chinese classics were too deep for us. After the establishment of the Republic, they started a new style of teaching.

The classics were very prosaic. In the Chinese countryside, they held on to the old style of learning. If you wanted to get a modern education, you had to go to the city.

My paternal aunt and maternal grandmother lived in Gaoxian. I was sent to live with them and receive the so-called modern education. In these schools, which were divided into grade levels (ancient Chinese schools did not have grades), we had some new books, but the teachers still taught using outmoded methods. In fact, the so-called modern education was not all that modern. . . .

Question: Why are you now writing your memoirs?

Yein: In recent years, many people have been writing memoirs. Memoirs are really a record of a person's life in relation to actual historical events. I had a friend who just passed away. He did not write a memoir and therefore posterity forgot him. My fellow colleagues in arms got together and tried to compile our accomplishments. When we were doing this, I did not intend to write memoirs. Instead, I think it is important to let my offspring know what I have done in my life and where I came from. I do not refer to my memoirs as "memoirs" in the usual sense of recording one's accomplishments. It is really an autobiography entitled "I." People who have had notable public careers write "memoirs." I really only want family to read mine.

Reading Between the Lines: History Within History

Rarely do words contain only one level of meaning. Usually when people speak to you, they are working from a set of assumptions. After having compiled the oral history, I found the process of transcription equally frustrating because I simply did not undertand the context in which my grandfather was speaking.

As the genealogist, you will need to get your bearings straight. Think of yourself as a ship's captain navigating an unknown sea. Anything your subject says is potentially meaningful. The more I studied Chinese history, the more my grandfather's words carried substance.

Like many young men during the 1920s, Grandfather believed that China needed to be saved. His beliefs were idealistic. His words, charged with patriotism, are characteristic of his generation:

> We printed four phrases on our military uniforms. The first was "Love your country." Even though these words were simple, most soldiers did not understand them, much less did they who were warlords. A warlord's soldier is not a soldier of the country. What was the second phrase? It was "Love the masses." When soldiers set up camp at night, they often stayed in people's houses, causing them a great deal of trouble. The students of our academy believed that these people were like our own family, just like sisters and brothers. "Love your country," "Love the masses," "Love not money," and "Fear not death."

Every background history I could read about China during the 1920s intensified the meaning of my grandfather's words. As you broaden your knowledge base, it is easy to stray from your original intent. Let your mind wander, let your project undergo metamorphosis, but keep good notes and try to focus on one thought at a time. Finding someone to interview and transcribing the interview should be a very interesting project in and of itself. Do not become discouraged by things that seem initially hard to understand.

Many of us have wondered where we came from. In doing an oral history, ask your relatives about the history of the family. As I came to know my grandfather better, I realized that he was surrounded by clues of his own search to reconcile his existence with the past. When interviewing a Chinese relative, ask about material objects that might be meaningful to the person; perhaps a painting, a book, or a scroll. Many Chinese hang calligraphy on the wall not only for artistic reasons, but also to convey personal philosophies.

My grandfather's personal motto, "Mountains high, waters eternal," was in fact a eulogy to the hermit he considered to be his family's founding ancestor. Anthropologists call this kind of forebear an eponymic ancestor. This means that we cannot prove whether or not the ancestor is truly related to the person who adopts the ancestor. People often adopt eponymic ancestors when they are seeking significance in their own lives. Eponymic ancestors usually serve as exemplars to the generation that adopts them.

I asked Grandfather to tell me more about Sir Yein, his eponymic ancestor. His face lit up and he immediately went to look for Sir Yein's eulogy written by a T'ang Dynasty official:

> Sir Yein was the longtime friend of Emperor Guang Wu-ti.
>
> The two were friends by virtue of principle: both believed in morality and loyalty. When Guang Wu-ti grasped the red flag [became emperor] and became the Son of Heaven, he gained the company of saintly officials. Who could possibly surpass the emperor?
>
> Only Sir Yein could. The two slept in the same company which stirred the heavens. Sir Yein went to Fu Chun River to lead a hermetic life. He gained pure virtue and threw away his worldly position and glory. Under the sky, is there one to surpass him?

I could now understand why my grandfather, a seasoned military official, might admire the virtuous Sir Yein. Sir Yein rejected the corruption of politics for an untainted life devoted to upholding moral principles.

Learning as Much as You Can

Oral history is not just a matter of interviewing someone and transcribing their responses. Creating a meaningful oral history is an interactive process. It requires planning and organizing. Try to broaden your perspective. Ask yourself what characteristics your subject might share with others of his or her generation. Although we like to think of ourselves as unique individuals, we are in many ways affected by larger trends and waves in the history of humankind. Unless our relatives were real hermits, they have shared a similiar set of experiences with their peers.

Grandfather was a politically motivated young man; in fact, many of his generation had strong political beliefs. This period in his life might be compared to the 1960s in the United States, when many young people were motivated by ideals and transformed their beliefs into actions.

Oral history allows us to understand the larger trends in history at a personal level. From your oral history, you can branch out in many directions.

Chinese Memoirs

Creativity can add exciting dimensions to your genealogy project. Let's say that you have stumbled upon an ancestor who particularly interests you. Perhaps you have found that this ancestor was related to a prominent historical figure. Perhaps this ancestor was a humble farmer. No matter what walk of life your ancestors came from, they were each living, breathing people who lived through many experiences. If your ancestors were unable to leave a trail of paper—written records—for you to follow, you will need to use a great deal of imagination to fill in the gaps. Once in a while, you may be so fortunate as to obtain an ancestor's autobiography.

Chinese memoirs (*hui i lu*) are fascinating sources. Anybody, famous or not, can write *hui i lu*. Similar to autobiographies written in other cultures, *hui i lu* are written usually in the first person. A *hui i lu* documents a person's life from his own perspective. This perspective is called the "first person." For all intents and purposes, *hui i lu* are Chinese autobiographies. Rarely does one use the term *zi zhuan*, or literally "autobiography." Even if the *hui i lu* was not actually composed by the individual, it is written in a style that is intended to make the reader feel that he or she has entered the realm of the first person.

Chinese memoirs use the vernacular instead of classical Chinese and, compared to many sources introduced in this book, are relatively easy to read.

The examples in this chapter illustrate the fact that *hui i lu* can be written by almost anyone; they can be written by famous people, and by not-so-famous people. As examples, I have selected the *hui i lu* of the last Chinese emperor, and another *hui i lu* written by the wife of a Chinese official. Many *hui i lu* never get published and are simply distributed among family members. We will detail and discuss the overall format of a *hui i lu* and translate key passages to give you a feeling for their style.

Memoirs of Madame Zhang Guoxun: *The Past Is Smoke*

Many of the sources introduced to you in this volume have been biased in their representation of gender. As you know, ancient Chinese genealogical sources such as the *zupu* concentrated on males because they were written to support the patriarchal system of inheritance.

The twentieth century brought education to many Chinese women. As a result, women writers became far more prolific. During the 1930s and 1940s, many female novelists became well known for their works that called for social reform. Although many Chinese women remained illiterate, women had better opportunities for education.

Educated women who achieved social prominence either by their own merits or through their marriages could express themselves by writing memoirs, or *hui i lu*. In *The Past Is Smoke*, Madame Zhang Guoxun writes about her life as a young revolutionary of the early twentieth century. She and her husband, Zhang Guoxun, were deeply involved in Chinese politics during an era of turmoil. Chinese monarchy no

This young Chinese woman was a member of the Chinese Red Army in 1941. Women participated in welfare and propaganda activities for the Communist Party, rather than taking part in combat.

longer existed after the Revolution of 1911. The lack of a political center caused many idealistic youth of the day to dedicate their lives to saving China from complete anarchy.

Although Madame Zhang personally lived through important historical events, her memoirs are written in a very personal style. The following is a translation of her foreword:

> I am not a feminine woman. Ever since youth, I have acted like an unbridled man, doing everything in broad strokes. My writing style displays this attitude.
>
> Writing this book has been a catharsis: it is as if I have released many years of pent-up emotions. The book highlights several turning points in my life from the time I enrolled in the Communist Party (age nineteen), to the War of Resistance (age thirty-seven). [The War of Resistance refers to the conflict between the Chinese and Japanese in World War II.] Those who read this book might be able to piece together the historical fragments of China's political development. I was born in Hubei, in a small town located at the secluded northwestern corner of the province. A woman who grew up in a feudalistic society such as myself might easily fall into deep despair. I would hope to inspire in my readers the desire to always improve themselves. I would also like to remind people of the suffering and inequalities women of my time were subjected to.
>
> After having been influenced by the new style of thinking and having been pulled into the vortex of the Communist Movement, I became a cadre. The fact that I loved arts and literature did not mean that I blindly followed the political trends. After marriage, I thirsted for a normal life, a place where love could abound.
>
> My innate character is to be straightforward. In my naïveté, I could not accept those schemers who were out for their own gain.
>
> I met my husband, Zhang Guoxun, who had left the Communist Party, during the War of Resistance. I began to sympathize with him and did the same. My whole being

felt comforted at this new-found freedom. The past thirty years since the War have been quite difficult at times, but in general, I feel at ease and content with my life.

Madame Zhang's memoir gives us a sense of how vast historical transformation affects people at a personal level. Madame Zhang's generation is probably that of either your grandparents or great-grandparents.

It is important to view the creation of *hui i lu* as a literary trend. Before the fall of the last Chinese emperor in 1911, classical Chinese was the accepted language of public communication. Many literary critics and academics of the day advocated the use of modern Chinese as we know it today. Their impact on literature was great: the result was acceptance of a more colloquial language that could be understood by a larger audience. Historical circumstance made the proliferation of the *hui i lu* possible.

Pu Yi's Autobiography

As discussed earlier, historical transformation affects the way people view themselves in society. Autobiography as a literary genre is new for almost any culture. In the past, those considered commoners rarely were mentioned in historical documents. In China, memoirs and autobiographies became widespread during the twentieth century, however.

Pu Yi was the last emperor of China. His autobiography shows that even members of the imperial family were affected by social change, change vaster than even they could fathom. Pu Yi's autobiography is a hybrid of the personal memoir and family history. The writing style is vernacular and remarkably informal in tone for royalty.

Pu Yi does not begin with himself, but rather with his ancestry. He dedicates the first few sections of the autobiography to his grandparents, and the infamous Empress Dowager, who was known to have been the actual power behind the throne. Only after the introduction of elders does Pu Yi begin to tell the audience about himself.

It is doubtful that the autobiography was solely authored by Pu Yi himself. Although the style of writing seems informal, it becomes evident that the autobiography is meant to portray Pu Yi's life as it was affected by the fate of the last dynasty. Below is an excerpt:

My Youth: Ascending and Descending the Throne

It was during the thirty-fourth year of the Guangxu emperor that a large uprising took place in the quarters of Xun Wang. Fu Jin passed out before having even heard the official decree of the Empress brought over by Zheng Wang. The elders of the family who later relayed this portion of history to me are now but ghosts of my past. I have no impression of them. In fact, we owe it to a wet nurse who completed the story for us. The wet nurse saw me crying and breast-fed me. Soothed, I stopped crying. This sequence of events aroused the attention of the now powerless elders. The Imperial guards and my father consulted one another and made a decision. The wet nurse would carry me to Zhongnanhai and once there would present me to the Empress Dowager, Cixi Taihou.

When I met with Cixi this time, we both could vaguely recall what had happened. I remember that I was suddenly surrounded by a horde of strangers. In front of us there was a luxuriant curtain out from which peeped a dour face. This was Cixi. It is said that when I first met Cixi, I cried with abandon. The Guards quaked. Cixi ordered one of the attendants to fetch some rock candy which I threw to the ground. I cried out, "I want Mother!" This made the Empress Dowager extremely angry. She said, "This child is a nuisance. Take him to play at once!"

On the third day of my arrival at the palace, the Empress Dowager passed away. After about a month, my ascension to the throne took place. My carrying on and crying disrupted the solemnity of the occasion. . . .

In his autobiography, Pu Yi is frequently anecdotal. His use of the vernacular style rather than classical Chinese is a sign of diluted imperial power. It comes as no surprise that Pu Yi was China's last monarch.

Madame Nien Cheng celebrates her new U.S. citizenship at the Statue of Liberty in 1988. She had survived seven years in Chinese prisons and wrote a memoir about her experiences called *Life and Death in Shanghai*.

Autobiography and Genealogy

As sources, autobiographies make a mere name come to life. If you are lucky enough to get your hands on a memoir, you may find references to other ancestors nestled among the lines of self-portrayal. When using autobiographies for genealogical material, have pen and paper ready. Note unfamiliar terms and people. These will be your road signs to other places. While it is easy to become engrossed in one person's story, always think about the subject's historical context.

Although you are not an emperor of China, the events in your life are no less important to future genealogists than are those of Pu Yi. Imagine how wonderful it would be if you could find memoirs for every one of your relatives, every woman who worked in the New York garment district, every man who mined for gold in California. If you begin now to write down memories of your life and the times you live in, it will be a great gift to your children and grandchildren. We will discuss autobiography in more detail in the following chapter.

Resources

ORAL HISTORY

Allen, Barbara, and Montell, William Lynwood. *From Memory to History: Using Oral Sources in Local Historical Research.* **Nashville, TN: American Association for State and Local History, 1981.**

> This text is extremely helpful for those who have already gathered oral histories and are interested in writing a family history based on that material.

Arthur, Stephen, and Arthur, Julia. *Your Life & Times: How to Put a Life Story on Tape.* **Baltimore: Genealogical Publishing Co., 1987.**

> Provides you with a list of questions that will lead you through your personal history, and advises you on how to record an oral history.

Banaka, William H. *Training in Depth Interviewing.* **New York: Harper & Row, 1971.**

> Helps you keep your interviews organized and focused. Includes tips on preparation, effective questions to use, and strategies for getting the information you want from the interviewee.

Bannister, Shala Mills. *Family Treasures: Videotaping Your Family's History. A Guide for Preserving Your Family's Living History as an Heirloom for Future Generations.* **Baltimore: Clearfield Co., 1994.**

> A guide to videotaping your family history, with advice on interviewing.

Davis, Cullom; Back, Kathryn; and Maclean, Kay. *Oral History: From Tape to Type.* **Chicago: American Library Association, 1977.**

Contains information on interviewing, transcribing, and editing oral history data. Also gives helpful tips on note-taking and organization of interviews.

Deering, Mary Jo, and Pomeroy, Barbara. *Transcribing Without Tears: A Guide to Transcribing and Editing Oral History Interviews*. Washington, DC: Oral History Program, George Washington University Library, 1976.

Transcribing is a time-consuming and tedious but necessary part of oral history interviews. What do you do when an interviewee leaves a sentence dangling, starts a subject but never really answers your question, or finally answers it while talking about another subject ten minutes later? Consult this book for advice on dealing with these common problems.

Fletcher, William P. *Record Your Family History*. Berkeley, CA: Ten Speed Press, 1989.

Explains how to preserve your family's oral history on videotape and audiotape. It suggests interview techniques, includes sample questions, and gives examples of what to listen for when interviewing.

Garner, Van Hastings. *Oral History: A New Experience in Learning*. Dayton, OH: Pflaum Publishing, 1975.

Contains chapters on organization, technique, and style for the interview. Bibliography included.

Harvey, Joanne H. *The Living Record: Interviewing and Other Techniques for Genealogists*. Lansing, MI: J. H. Harvey, 1985.

Harvey provides advice on conducting interviews. Her suggestions are geared specifically to genealogists.

Hoopes, James. *Oral History: An Introduction for Students*. Chapel Hill: University of North Carolina Press, 1979.

Contains chapters on arranging, preparing, and conducting interviews. Also has a listing of oral history collections and sources in the bibliography.

Ives, Edward I. *The Tape-Recorded Interview: A Manual for Field Workers in Folklore and Oral History.* **Knoxville: University of Tennessee Press, 1974.**

Although the information on the use of tape recorders is a bit out of date, the chapters on interviewing techniques and making a transcript may be of interest. Includes sample edited oral history manuscripts, letters, and release forms.

McLaughlin, Paul. *A Family Remembers.* **North Vancouver, BC: Self-Counsel Press, 1993.**

A fine guide to creating a family history with video cameras and tape recorders. Includes tips on lighting, acoustics, interviewing, and editing.

Schumacher, Michael. *Creative Conversations: The Writer's Complete Guide to Conducting Interviews.* **Cincinnati: Writer's Digest Books, 1990.**

The first chapter, entitled "The Interview and Its Uses," is particularly helpful. Contains many useful tips for both the writer and the family historian.

Shumway, Gary L., and Hartley, William G. *An Oral History Primer.* **Salt Lake City: Shumway, 1973.**

The authors explain the significance of oral history to family heritage. They also tell you what to do with the tales and songs once you have recorded them.

Stano, Michael E., and Reinsch, Jr., N. L. *Communication in Interviews.* **Englewood Cliffs, NJ: Prentice-Hall, 1982.**

Although this is a general guide to interviewing, its points can be easily applied to a genealogical interview. Topics discussed include: preparation, strategies for communicating clearly, and how to read verbal and nonverbal signals.

Sturm, Duane, and Sturm, Pat. *Video Family History.*
Salt Lake City: Ancestry, Inc., 1989.

If you have the opportunity to borrow a video camera, try recording your oral history interviews and compiling them in a video documentary of your family history. The authors provide tips on equipment and techniques such as editing and dubbing.

Thompson, Paul. *The Voice of the Past: Oral History.*
New York: Oxford University Press, 1978.

The chapter on "the interview" is especially helpful, with tips on ordering and phrasing questions. Also includes many example questions.

Zhang, Xinxin, and Sang, Ye. *Chinese Lives: An Oral History of Contemporary China.* **New York: Pantheon, 1987.**

The voices of a broad spectrum of Chinese people form a vivid portrait of Chinese society. A thirteen-year-old boy, a prison guard, a bus conductor, and a pop singer are among the people interviewed by the authors, both journalists. As you read, you will get a sense of the exciting flavor of oral history.

Chapter 8
Your Final Result

Writing a Family History

Some people find writing a daunting task. If this describes you, you may want to take your family history in small steps. Begin by writing about one relative. Write one paragraph about the person who interests you most. Where did she come from, when, and why? What did she look like? Whom did she marry? Did she have children? Did she work? How did she die and where was she buried? Do you have any of her letters, or stories about her from living relatives?

If you approach each ancestor in this way, writing the answer to one question at a time, you will be surprised how steadily your family history grows. Remember to document exactly where you found each piece of information, such as whether it came from a birth certificate or was told as a family joke by your grandfather.

Your family history can be greatly enhanced with illustrations. These may be old photos, sketches, or any other portrayal of your ancestors. Photographs are the best accompaniment to a written account of your roots. They may be recent photos that you or a relative has taken of ancestral homes, old churches or schools, or heirlooms that once belonged to your ancestors. The story of an ancestor's voyage to the United States will be even more moving if it is accompanied by a picture of the beautiful silk robe he carried with him to this country, although he never wore it again.

Such heirlooms are precious records of your ancestors as human beings. Keeping a list of what you find and who is keeping it will mean a lot to your family. As your relatives grow old and die, you can make sure that the family heirlooms are saved and respected. No matter how you choose to use your genealogical research, you are making an important contribution to coming generations of your family, and to the Chinese American community. Taking pride in your family line is a part of your heritage. You come from a culture that has practiced the art of genealogy for millennia.

Writing Your Autobiography

You may think that you would have little to write about in an autobiography—or, at least, little that would be of interest to future generations. But don't be so sure. Wouldn't you enjoy reading about even the most mundane details in the lives of your ancestors—what they ate, what they wore, what they studied in school? These everyday details can sometimes be just as interesting, or even more so, than accounts of major events.

Start by writing down some basic information about yourself, such as where and when you were born, how many siblings you have, what you are doing in school, who your friends are, and what you enjoy doing with them. Try describing a typical day in your life, from morning until evening. Describe what your house and room are like. What are some important events in your life? For example, how did you feel when a new sibling was born or when a much-loved older relative died?

Write about your experience as a Chinese American. Do you feel different from your classmates? Have you ever experienced discrimination or racism? What are some aspects of your Chinese American heritage that are particularly meaningful to you? Do you speak Chinese? With whom?

You may want to include your autobiography with your written family history. Continue adding to it as your life changes, or whenever you feel like writing. Update it when you move to a new school, take an exciting trip, or make new friends, for example.

No one knows you like you do. As you list facts about yourself—where you were born, where you have lived, where you have gone to school—be sure to mix in feelings and opinions. Who was your best friend? How did you feel the first time you moved to a new school? What do you dream of doing in the future? How do you feel about world events that you hear about on the news? Any information you give about yourself will be a gold mine to family historians trying to get to know you in 150 years.

Genealogy and Computers

Computers can be very helpful when putting together your family history. They can lead you to sources of information as well as help you to organize your information in a useful and attractive way.

There are an increasing variety of computer software programs designed specifically for genealogists. They often include features such as cross-indexing and provide predesigned formats into which your own family's information can be inserted. Some programs allow you to insert images of your family next to their biographical information, and they will compile and edit the information you enter into a narrative format. They will also make it easier to set up and fill out pedigree charts, family group sheets, and family trees.

The Church of Jesus Christ of Latter-day Saints developed one of the first genealogical software packages, Personal Ancestral File (PAF). Its Family Records program allows you to enter genealogical information on your ancestors and organizes it into chart form.

While you must, of course, make sure that all of the information you enter is accurate, these computer programs can make it much easier to put your research into a form that can be read and enjoyed by other family members.

Resources

PREPARING YOUR WRITTEN FAMILY HISTORY

Banks, Keith E. *How to Write Your Personal and Family History: A Resource Manual.* **Bowie, MD: Heritage Books, 1988.**

Consult this guide for advice on putting your family history into writing.

Barnes, Donald R., and Lackey, Richard S. *Write It Right: A Manual for Writing Family Histories and Genealogies.* **Ocala, FL: Lyon Press, 1983.**

No one has set a standard for Chinese American genealogies. A traditional Chinese genealogy may not be the best format for you. Barnes and Lackey believe there are many things you can do with the information you gather.

Gouldrup, Lawrence P. *Writing the Family Narrative.* **Salt Lake City: Ancestry, Inc., 1987.**

Gouldrup shows the genealogist how to put his or her work into an interesting and readable format that can be enjoyed by all family members.

Jordan, Lewis. *Cite Your Sources: A Manual for Documenting Family Histories and Genealogical Records.* **Jackson: University Press of Mississippi, 1980.**

Citing your sources will add legitimacy to your project. This book gives advice on how to make citations clear for a variety of genealogical sources.

ILLUSTRATING YOUR FAMILY HISTORY

Earnest, Russell D. *Grandma's Attic: Making Heir-*

looms Part of Your Family History. **Albuquerque, NM: R. D. Earnest Assoc., 1991.**

> This book advises you on what you should look for when exploring the family storage area, such as letters and diaries.

Frisch-Ripley, Karen. *Unlocking Secrets in Old Photos*. **Salt Lake City: Ancestry, Inc., 1991.**

> Explains how to date photos, identify faces in pictures, and restore old photos. Also includes guidance on using photos in a family tree or other genealogical presentation.

AUTOBIOGRAPHY

Kanin, Ruth. *Write the Story of Your Life*. **Baltimore: Clearfield Co., 1993.**

> A thorough introduction to writing autobiography. Kanin discusses how to get the creative process started using various exercises, and includes examples from her own life to illustrate how to put the autobiography together. The book also contains a list of suggested readings.

GENEALOGICAL SOFTWARE

Ancestral File Operations Unit
50 North West Temple Street
Salt Lake City, UT 84150
801-240-2584

> Write for information on the Personal Ancestral File (PAF) from the Family History Library.

Banner Blue Software
P.O. Box 7865
Fremont, CA 94537
510-795-4490

Write or call for information on the Biography Maker software program. This program allows you to write one ancestor's story at a time and to tie several stories together with writing and history aids.

Commsoft, Inc.
7795 Bell Road
P.O. Box 310
Windsor, CA 95495-0130

Write for information on their Roots IV software program, which allows for different approaches to entry of genealogical data.

Dollarhide Systems
203 Holly Street
Bellingham, WA 28225
801-298-5358

Write or call for information on Everyone's Family Tree software, which is easy for beginners to learn.

Przecha, Donna, and Lowrey, Joan. *Guide to Genealogy Software*. Baltimore: Genealogical Publishing Co., 1993.

Genealogical software can be expensive; it's important not to jump into a purchase without making sure that the program will suit your needs. This book will help you make the right choice. The authors review dozens of software programs and utilities. Charts and illustrations show you what the software actually looks like on screen.

Glossary

cadre Group of indoctrinated leaders active in promoting a revolutionary party; a member of a cadre.

concubine An unmarried woman who lives in a household and holds a social status below that of the wife.

coolie The term used to refer to Chinese peasants who worked abroad as indentured servants. The term was also applied to Chinese railroad workers in the United States, even though they were not indentured servants.

credit-ticket system Another name for the coolie trade system, wherein Chinese peasants worked as indentured servants.

deed A written record of a land purchase.

dynasty An era marked by the rule of one dominant family and/or its blood relations.

eponymic ancestor An ancestor who cannot be traced to a particular family line with certainty, but is claimed as an ancestor by the family because he represents certain ideals.

extraterritoriality Exemption from the jurisdiction of local law; used to describe the situation when China was forced to give up certain areas to foreign economic and political control in the late nineteenth and early twentieth centuries.

grantor/grantee Terms used on legal documents; the grantor is someone who sells land; the grantee is someone who buys land.

honorific Title used in referring to a social superior.

ideograms Symbols used in various languages to represent ideas or objects.

imperial   Royal; often used when describing an emperor or his family.

literati   Formally educated people of ancient China, often elite members of society and the compilers of genealogies.

paper sons   Young men illegally brought to the United States after the 1906 earthquake in California destroyed many immigration and naturalization records.

romanization   The way Chinese characters are rendered in the Roman alphabet. There are many systems of romanization, including Pinyin and Wade Giles.

Three Knives   Name used to describe the main Chinese American occupations in the mid-nineteenth century—restaurant, tailor shop, and laundry owners. The name refers to the misery that these workers associated with such jobs.

tong   In China, a meeting hall; in the United States, the term was used by Chinese immigrants to describe secret fraternal organizations established to protect them from discrimination.

vesting document   Recorded document that officially transfers property ownership or title from one party to another.

vital records   Official documents that record significant dates such as birth, death, and marriage.

Warlord Period   An era when various groups, led by military strongmen, established their own military fortifications in China's provinces.

Chinese Genealogical Terms

bai jia   The 100 households that appear most often in Chinese genealogies. Palace officials were selected from these households.

di fang zhi   Local gazetteers containing valuable information about China's diverse regions, much of it useful to genealogists.

di zhang zhi   A term used during the Zhou Dynasty to

refer to the eldest son in a family. The term was significant because the eldest son had access to many special rights and privileges.

die Biographical sketches found within a *zupu*.

Han The largest Chinese ethnic group. Also refers to the dynasty that ruled 206 BC–220 AD.

hui i lu Personal memoirs.

jia Household, house, or family. This term can refer to the members of a household as well as the physical house.

pu Genealogical name charts found within a *zupu*.

pu jin The imperial ban on compiling genealogies, in effect during the Ch'ing Dynasty.

zhu hou Chinese feudal prince whose power came from a blood relation to the imperial family.

zupu Clan register, the Chinese form of a family history or genealogy. The *zupu* is usually bound as a book and contains information about the members of each generation of a family. *Pu* and *die* are elements of the zupu.

Chinese Kinship Terms (Mandarin)

biao di Younger male cousin from paternal or maternal side (different last name).

biao ge Older male cousin from paternal or maternal side (with different last name).

biao jie Older female cousin from paternal or maternal side (different last name).

biao mei Younger female cousin (different last name).

bo-bo Paternal uncle (older than father).

fumu Parents.

gu-ma Paternal aunt.

jiemei Sisters.

jiujiu Maternal uncle.

shu-shu Paternal uncle (younger than father).

tang di Young male cousin from paternal side (with same last name).

tang ge Older male cousin from paternal side (with same last name).

tang jie Older female cousin from paternal side (with same last name).

tang mei Younger female cousin from paternal side (with same last name).

waigoing Affectionate term for maternal grandfather.

waipo Affectionate term for maternal grandmother.

waizufu Formal term for maternal grandfather.

waizumu Formal term for maternal grandmother.

xiongdi Brothers.

yeh-yeh Affectionate term for paternal grandfather.

yima Maternal aunt.

zufu Formal term for paternal grandfather.

zumu Formal term for paternal grandmother.

Index

ABOUT THE AUTHOR
Colleen She received a master's degree in East Asian studies from Columbia University. She is a free-lance writer and translator.

ILLUSTRATION CREDITS
Cover, © David W. Hamilton/The Image Bank; cover inset and pp. viii, 3, 5, 17, 20, 24, 27, 32, 34, 40, 63, 65, 82, 84, 110, 131, 144, 148, BETTMANN. *Color insert*: p. 2, 6, 16, AP/Wide World Photos; p. 3, 4, 5, 7, 8, 9, 14, 15, BETTMANN; p. 10, © David W. Hamilton/The Image Bank; p. 11, © Tom McKitterick/ Impact Visuals; p. 12, © Rick Gerharter/Impact Visuals; p. 13, © Ken Martin/ Impact Visuals.

LAYOUT AND DESIGN
Kim Sonsky